Becoming Bereans
Bible Study

Becoming Bereans Bible Study

A Bible study designed to encourage the whole family to understand and apply the Word of God.

Corby Shuey

Becoming Bereans Bible Study / Corby Shuey
ISBN: 9798848396065

[10] The brethren immediately sent Paul and Silas away by night to Berea, [a]and when they arrived, they went into the synagogue of the Jews. [11] Now these were more noble-minded than those in Thessalonica, [b]for they received the word with [c]great eagerness, examining the Scriptures daily to see whether these things were so. [12] Therefore many of them believed, [d]along with a number of prominent Greek women and men.

—Acts 17:10-12 NASB95

Contents

Acknowledgments

This Bible Study was originally written to be utilized as part of a family Bible study series at Mount Zion Road Church. I thank the congregation of Mount Zion Road Church for allowing me to both write and facilitate this study. It was no small endeavor. I am grateful for your trust in my leadership.

I also thank those who participated. The purpose of the study is to equip those who know Jesus as Lord and Savior with the wisdom to stand firmly planted on His eternal Word. Most importantly, to share your faith with those who you have the opportunity to be a witness. I pray that the study was edifying. I pray that you were equipped to stand strong and be like the Bereans who received the Word with eagerness and examined truth daily.

To God be the glory!

The Purpose for the Study

In the beginning, God created the heavens and the Earth. He created Adam and Eve. He created a family. He gave them a home. He gave them structure and rules. He imparted a set of expectations upon them. In the beginning, God wanted to be a Father and have communion with his children. Unfortunately, we were deceived. Adam failed to uphold the expectations. Through Adam, we have inherited an innate proclivity to sin. We are all guilty. We failed to protect God's home, and we were stolen away by sin.

The rest of the Bible is a command. It is a command that describes the actions that God will enact to get his family back. I chose the word command, because God's plan is not an IF or a MAYBE situation. God's word is an illustration of that command of redemption. He will restore His family.

When God created us, He wanted to have a relationship with us. The evidence of God's desire to have fellowship with us can be seen at the very beginning of the Bible. The Hebrew word which was translated to "In the beginning," is the word *Bereshith*. Jewish scholars debate as to why God chose to begin His word using the letter B. As you may know, the Hebrew language is a pictorial language. Each letter has a meaning that goes beyond simple phonetic mechanics. Each letter of the language also carries symbolic meaning. The Hebrew letter B represents the concept of home. What God is saying by using a word beginning with letter B, is that He created a home for us. He wants to dwell in fellowship with us.

When we sinned, we chose to inherit a sinful nature. We chose to become something that was not part of God's original plan. In doing this, we were no longer able to walk with God the same way anymore. Sin separated us from a right relationship with Him. As a result of our decision to sin, God is working to redeem us and restore us to his family.

With this in mind, we have to ask ourselves: do we seek to create a home that is inviting to God? In our families, are we working to accommodate our most esteemed guest? Are we working to stand upon the purity of His Word?

We all recognize that the world is changing and consequently the church, at least in part is following suit. The Bible believing church is under attack due to our cultural unrest. We need more, bigger, better. Just taking the word of God seriously is old fashioned. We need flashy worship and wishy-washy theology. The church is asked to bend and compromise. The church is what needs to become more tolerant. The church is judgmental. The word sin does not carry the same weight anymore. Sin is almost seen as a mistake or an OOPS moment. The innocence of the church is being called to question. The church, in own present day, is being convicted, tried and sentenced without committing a crime. Just as in the last days of the Messiah, the world is demanding a condemnation of death upon the church. Either compromise and stop proclaiming the word of God so loudly or go away. Unfortunately, parts of God's church are compromising. Parts of God's church are tolerating. Parts of God's church are editing the very word of God to meet the demands of sinners. Church is becoming a place that is not welcoming to God. I wonder, is God's home moving away from the church, like God moved away from the temple during the conquest of Babylon?

Why is this happening? Why are we allowing the world to bend the rules that were so clearly given in God's word? Many church leaders blame this trend, in the church, to bend toward tolerance to the fact that so many believers are "Biblically Illiterate." We possess only a weak grasp on what the Word says. In our frail knowledge of the Word, we present ourselves with no defense. We allow the world to infiltrate our church services maybe because we do not know any better.

"Biblical Illiteracy" is taking a significant even devastating toll on the viability of the church. Research conducted by the Pew Research Center found that

"49%"[1] of young people, who claim to be raised in the church, fall away in their early adult life. The research cited that "a lack of belief led them to move away from religion."[2] Our children are so indoctrinated by the way of the world, that they have no defense against secular influences. Our children have grown up being fed secular apologetics but not given anything to help them defend their faith in the One True God.

Our culture is pushing us to relinquish our control. We are being conditioned to simply accept the ways of the world and move on. This trend has also seeped into the church. Many believers think that it is the job of the Sunday School Teacher and the Pastor to train up the children in the ways of the Lord. Most of the ministry in the church is left to those in charge; the majority of the congregants sit back and enjoy the ride. Have we become complacent and comfortable with just attending church for an hour or two and then not thinking about it again until next Sunday? Are we teaching our children that church is something that you need to **<u>endure</u>** once a week? Jesus tells us in the Gospel of Matthew that "The bridegroom was a long time in coming, and they all became drowsy and fell asleep." In this verse, Jesus is talking about the church. The church became tired of waiting for Jesus to return and they all fell asleep. Satan is happy to lull us to sleep in the pew as long as we are not awake and working to build the kingdom of God.

Let me explain the vision of this Bible study. We help our children with their school homework. When we help them with their homework we are teaching them that we think it is important. It is worthy of investing the time to work on together. Why not help them understand God's word the same way? Why not work together and do God's homework? Why not show them that studying the Bible together is important? It is not about what we say; it is about how we live.

---

[1] Lipka, Michael. "Why America's 'nones' left religion behind." pewresearchcenter.org. Pew Research Center, 24 August, 2016. Accessed on May 16, 2017.

[2] Ibid.

I know that I have been talking a lot about parents and children. I have just been using this as an illustration that we can all relate to. I think we need to wake up the church as a whole. Too many have been lulled to sleep and given others the responsibility of spiritual education. Too many say, "Someone else will do that. It is not my responsibility." We need to do something. We need to wake up the church. We need to teach people how to have church in their own hearts, how to welcome God back into their own homes. We need to hold each other accountable for learning and teaching God's word to our families. Traditionally, Hebrew families read from the Bible together in their homes. The parents were the teachers of the Law. Each family was assigned a Levite. The Levite would mentor and clarify the teaching of the parents to make sure they are following the word of God. This was how church services were conducted, in the home, together. Don't be alarmed; I am not saying that we need to get rid of our church. What I am saying is that, we need to bring the word of God back home. We should learn how to have church all week long in our homes. The Sunday service should be the glorious punctuation at the end of the spirit filled sentence.

I purpose that we take a new look at studying the Bible. I think that God is calling us to draw together, to seek out the face of God as a family. God is calling His family back home. We need to get off of our spiritual couches and answer the call.

One step that we need to take is to bring the family together to study the Bible. Grandparents, parents and children, husband and wife, mother and children, sitting and reading the Holy Word of God together.

In Joel chapter 2 verse 16, God says: "Gather the people, consecrate the assembly; bring together the elders, gather the children, those nursing at the breast. Let the bridegroom leave his room and the bride her chamber." God is calling his people together to prepare for the coming of the Bridegroom. We need to study together. We need to read the Word together.

God's word also instructs us in Nehemiah chapter 8 verses 5-8: "Ezra opened the book. All the people could see him because he was standing above them; and as he opened it, the people all stood up. Ezra praised the Lord, the great God; and all the people lifted their hands and responded, 'Amen! Amen!' Then they bowed down and worshipped the Lord with their faces to the ground.

The Levites- Jeshua, Bani, Sherebiah, Jamin, Akkub, Shabbethai, Hodiah, Maaseiah, Kelita, Azariah, Jozabad, Hanan and Peaiah- instructed the people in the Law while the people were standing there. They read from the book of the law of God, making it clear and giving the meaning so that the people could understand what was being read."

We are to read the Word together and help those who do not understand find meaning. In the days in which we live, we need to stand together and proclaim God's kingdom as a family. Right now, it is our watch. Right now, is our opportunity to place Gods fingerprint on our lives. Right now, it is time to sharpen our swords so that we can stand and fight for the respect of God's Kingdom.

How This Study Will Work

This study will be difficult. This study will most likely be different than any other Bible study that you have done in the past. It is in completing the difficult things that we find true growth. This study is designed to help families and individuals grow in their understanding of God's Word. We are to be diligent in searching out the truth of the scripture. In our diligence, we will become Bereans.

I want to take the time to describe how this study works. Please read this section thoroughly, so that you have a firm grasp on how to proceed. First, I want to explain how the family study groups should look. I will then describe each aspect of the lessons.

I am going to proceed by assuming that most people participating will be involved in a larger group setting through a weekly Bible study at a church. Typically, in larger Bible studies, the adults will go to an adult class and the children will go to a children's group. This study is different in that it is designed to be done in smaller family groups. The most basic form of this would be the typical family structure of a Dad, Mom, and children. If grandparents are going to participate they would also be included in this group. The study is meant to be multigenerational with the parents leading the discussion to the group. The family group is to sit together, adults and children, to work through each lesson.

I know that not every group will fit into the traditional family structure category. In this case, group individuals as much as possible into groups which include both adults and children. Try to limit the size of each group to no more than eight people. Smaller groups will work batter, as it requires participation from everyone.

When the groups are established, you can proceed to work through the lessons. The point of the family grouping is to have the parents and adults be the facilitators of the study. Parents should be the source of teaching their children the truths of God's Word. As the groups go through the lesson, include the children into the discussions. Ask them to look up and read scripture. Ask them if they know what a specific word means. If they do not know what it means take the time to explain it to them. Ask them if they know who all of the are in a particular passage. If they do not know, take the time to explain. We, as adults, can learn so much by answering the questions of our children.

Use the notes in your Bible, or even you phone or laptop to help. The point of the study to understand what is being said in the Word. Talk thorough each passage of scripture to ensure that all members of the group understand what was written. Take your time, the idea is to delve deeply in understanding, not to simply get the study done.

The difficulty will be in the discussion and involvement of all members of the group. We are so accustomed to receiving information. In church, at school, even at home in front of the TV, we sit there and receive. The Word of God is alive and it is meant to be talked about. Do your best to talk to each other about the scripture and the questions related to the scripture. The learning comes in the discussion, not in the answer to the questions.

Lesson Format

I will now take a few moments to explain the format of the lessons. Each lesson is based on what God says about a particular topic. There are twelve lessons in this study. I organized the lessons based on how God reveals Himself to us. Initially we come to know God through His love. As we grow in our faith, we recognize His authority. Because of His authority, we adjust or personal walk, which influences our family life.

Each lesson is centered on a focus statement. The statement gives a brief synopsis of the intended learning. Read the focus to your group before you start. Explain any difficult words or concepts. Make sure everyone knows what the discussion will revolve around.

The heart of the lesson is in the scripture and associated questions. Look up each scripture. Assist the younger group members with finding the scripture. Part of the lesson is teaching younger members how to use their Bible.

Read the scripture aloud to the group. You can take turns reading, round robin style, or you can just pick someone to read the entire selection. Make sure to include the young group members. Allow them to read as much as possible.

After the reading, it may be necessary to ask if everyone understands what was written. Ask if everyone knows who and or what was happening in the verses read. Take the time to clarify and discuss anything that was not clear. You may also want to summarize the verses in your own words. Anyone in the group can do this to make the passage more vivid. **This step is essential for learning. DO NOT SKIP IT.**

When everyone understands, answer the associated questions for each passage of scripture. After adequate time for discussion move on to the next scripture. Continue until the allotted time is up.

In some lessons, you may find additional information to read to the group. This information is marked in bold. Read aloud to group.

Some groups may get a little farther in the study than other groups. It typically takes about 35 to 40 minutes to go through 5 verses of scripture and the questions for the scripture. Usually groups have time to answer sixteen or so questions. When the allotted time is up, mark where you stopped so that you can pick it back up the next time. Most lessons will take two sessions to complete.

At the end of each lesson there is a section called **"What does it all mean?"** This section consists of a group of summarizing questions. The questions are designed to bring the understanding of the whole lesson together. Some of the questions may require you to look up additional verses. Answer these questions as a group.

Two last things to point out. There is also a **"Mining for more"** section in each lesson. This section is written for adults to complete. The topics are a little more complex and may take more though to answer. This section should be completed after the rest of the lesson is finished. If time does not allow, please look at this section at home for homework.

The last aspect of each lesson is a page called **"Picturing the Passage."** On this page group members are required to draw a picture that relates to the learning. Children or adults can participate in this activity. Children can work on this while the adult members of the group discuss the Mining for More questions. Please do not allow children to begin this activity until all of the questions are complete.

When all of this is complete gather the whole group, if applicable, together and debrief any learning that was important. Or the larger group can answer questions that the smaller groups may still have. This can be brief.

Each lesson also has a craft or a game to be completed after the study. Depending on how your group is structured and how much time is allotted, will determine how this activity is completed. If you are doing this study at home, feel free to complete the extra activities to the best of your abilities. If you are meeting in a larger church setting, some initial prep work will be necessary to complete the craft and or game activity. The games do not require any special equipment other than a kick ball and dodge ball. The crafts will require general craft supplies such as: construction paper, markers, glue, things to make cards, etc... Nothing too fancy. A description of each activity is included after the lesson. The activities are also designed to enhance the learning.

It is essential to close the study with prayer.

Basic Study Structure

This schedule is just a suggestion. It can be changed to accommodate your group's needs.

- Praise and Worship music played as people enter
- (10 to 15 mins. Prior to the designated start time)
- Open with the singing of a Hymn
- Prayer for God's will.
- Into of topic: brief jumpstart and focus of lesson
- Individual family groups look up verses, answer questions about the verses.
- Take time as a family to define words and or concepts.
- Discuss findings as a whole group.
- Games or crafts
- Closing Prayer

Hebrews 4: 12-16

Becoming Bereans

Lesson One

Love

<u>Focus:</u> The Bible is a love story. God inspired over 40 authors to write 66 books containing 31,101 verses of scripture to communicate His unfailing love for us. I think God wants to make it clear that **we are His**. And as His children, He will stop at nothing to bless us in His promises. This lesson will focus on God's love. We will discuss how much God loves us, and what our response to this love should be.

Scripture: 1 John 4:7-8 (review and summarize verses. Restate the verse in your own words to help everyone to understand what God is saying.)

1. Where does love come from?

Scripture: Deuteronomy 7: 9 (remember to summarize verse.)

2. What is a covenant?

3. What is God's agreement or promise to us if we love Him and keep his commands?

Scripture Romans 6: 23

    4. Because God loves us so much, what gift does He want to give us?

Scripture: John 3:16

Read to group: All the way back in the Garden of Eden, we chose to sin. We chose to do something that God told us not to do. This choice made us sinners and separate from God's promises.

    5. What price was God willing to pay to get us back?
       (explain what Christ did for us if necessary)

Scripture: John 14: 23

    6. Describe what will happen if we choose to come under the payment that God has made for us. (What will happen if we obey Jesus?)

Our response to God's love

Scripture: Deuteronomy 10:12

    7. List the commands God gave us in this verse.

8. Name some things in your group that can show God that you love Him? (Each member of the group needs to list at least one.)

What does it all mean?

9. How do we know God? (Think back to the beginning of the study, in 1 John.)

10. It says in Romans that one of God's gifts to us is eternal life. How do we receive this gift?

11. Why does God want to give us such good gifts?

Mining for more: Read John 21: 15-17. In these verses, Jesus is giving Peter instruction on what is required if someone truly loves and wishes to follow Christ. Who are the sheep and lambs that Jesus is referring to? Where are those sheep and lambs found? What are we called to do to for them? How can we accomplish this task?

Picturing the Passage

Draw a picture about the love that God has for us.

Activity for Lesson 1: Love

This lesson was based on seeing God's love for us. The activity for this lesson will be to make a love card expressing our love for Him.

Materials Needed:

- Various colors of paper for the card
- Markers, crayons, colored pencils, or anything else to write or draw with
- Stickers, scrap paper, decorative papers, or anything decorative that can be applied to the card
- Glue

Procedure:

- Each person will make their own card
- Choose a piece of paper for the card. (Can be any size)
- Fold paper in half
- Write a note expressing how much you love God, or how much God has done for you inside the card
- Finish the card by decorating the cover

Keep the card as a reminder of the vast love that God has for His children

Lesson Two

Authority

Focus: Historically, we have held on to the fact that God is, was and ever will be the sovereign authority. He is the authority, which governs our personal lives as well as the essence of nature itself. But recently, the authority of God has been continually called into question. The world rejects God's authority. In this study, we will examine what God has written about the authority that He commands. We will also look at the authority given to Jesus and finally the authority given to us by God.

Scripture: Genesis 1:1- 27

(This reading is long, remember to stop and summarize as you read.)

1. What does God have the authority to command? Was anything written about that God did not have authority over?

2. If someone is able to give a command and nature itself obeys that command, what does this imply?

Scripture: Isaiah 43: 11- 13 (summarize verse)

3. Describe the authority that God claims for us in these verses?

4. Who are God's witnesses? What does a witness do?

5. Who is God claiming to be?

Scripture Psalm 89:33 – 37

6. Discuss the Hope that we have in God's authority. Go verse by verse talk about the promise found in each verse.

7. Discuss what God is talking about in verse 35.

Scripture: John 14: 9 - 10

8. By whose authority did Jesus walk?

9. If we walk like Jesus, what are the promises that we can claim?

Scripture: Mark 4: 36-41

10. How did Jesus show his authority?

11. Talk about what Jesus said in verse 40 of Mark 4. What is implied if we truly have faith? Hint: it has to do with confidence in someone?

12. What will our lives look like if we have complete confidence in Christ? How will our everyday routine change?

13. In verse 41, it states that even after Jesus calmed the storm the disciples were still terrified. Discuss reasons why they were still afraid.

Scripture: Leviticus 18: 1-5

14. Whose laws are we supposed to follow? Why does God give us laws? If we do not follow the laws given by an authority, what are we?

15. Why did God warn the Israelites not to follow the ways of the Egyptians and the Canaanites?

16. Do we follow any ways/trends/beliefs in our own culture that are apart from God? Explain your answer. Talk about this question with any children in your group. How does our culture try to trick us into not listening to God?

Scripture: 2 Samuel 22: 20- 22

17. If we submit to the authority of God, what is our blessing? There are a couple of things described.

READ TO GROUP: C. S. Lewis describes the fact that God wants to delight in us as "the weight of God's glory". God wants to pour out His glory on us, so that we can feel the heaviness of His truth and presence in our lives. Think about how heavy that idea is. The God of all creation wants to delight in us!

18. According to this passage, what do we need to do in order to find God's favor?

19. Discuss things that you can do in your life to cause God to delight in you.

Scripture: Luke 10: 19- 20

20. Name the things that we can overcome if we obey the authority of God.

21. What emotion does Jesus warn us about in verse 20?

What does it all mean?

22. How can we know that God's authority is real? There could be a number of answers to this question. If you get stuck, one response could be what we read about in the book of Genesis.

23. What happens when we move away from the authority of God?

24. We learned that there is only one sovereign authority and everlasting promise that we can rely on for the hope of deliverance, what steps can we take to give glory to our Deliverer?

Mining for more: There are two attributes of God that are seemingly on opposite ends of the spectrum: LAW and GRACE. What is the difference between the Law and Grace? Refer to the following verses: Exodus 13: 8, Exodus 24:12, Acts 15: 11, 1 Peter 5:10, Genesis 6:8-9, Genesis 6:22, Genesis 7:5. How does Grace compliment the Law?

Picturing the Passage

Draw a picture of people who have authority
(parents, teachers, policemen, doctors, pastors)

Activity for Lesson 2: Authority

There are essentially three competing sources to gain authority in our lives. One is God. The second is mankind, or ourselves. And the third is the enemy, satan. The activity will illustrate the levels of authority.

<u>Materials Needed</u>:
- This will be a group activity
- Each group will need a sheet of Blue, Green, and Red construction paper
- Each group will need markers, pencils or other things to write with.

<u>Procedure:</u>
- The 3 papers represent: Blue for God's authority, Green Man's authority, Red the lies of sin (what sin tells us we have authority to do.)
- On the blue paper, as a group, write down the things that God has authority over
- On the green paper, as a group, write the things that man has authority over
- On the red paper, as a group, write the things that sin tries to tell us that we have authority over. Write about how sin attempts to confuse our authority.
- The kids, or anyone, can decorate the papers to represent the various forms of authority that the papers represent.
- If time allows, the whole group can come together again and discuss what the small groups wrote

Hang all of the papers in your church, or homes as a reminder of an appropriate response to authority

Additional Activity for Lesson 2

Some of the studies may take more than one session to complete. In that case, I provided another activity. This is an activity for the second session for the lesson on **Authority.**

Materials Needed

- Bible
- Blindfold
- Area to play a game, basketball court, big open room, etc...

Procedure:

- One volunteer will represent the Word of God. This person will be holding the Bible.
- The person representing the Word of God will stand somewhere in the playing area. This person needs to stay at one place. No moving because the Word of God is unchanging.
- This person will be saying a favorite scripture verse over and over again. If a scripture verse does not come to mind, this person can repeat the phrase, "Word of God" over and over again as the game is being played.
- Another volunteer will be blindfolded.
- This person represents us, the everyday person.
- This person will listen for the Word of God and make his/her way to the Word.
- While the blindfolded person is trying to find the Word, other volunteers will represent sin.
- These people will try to block and distract the blindfolded person from finding the Word.

- Depending on the size of the group, you can adjust the number of players accordingly.
- After the person finds the Word, talk about why it is sometimes hard to find God's truth.
- If time allows play the game again. This time have the players change positions.
- Before plying a second time ask the group what everybody has available to them to help find the Word. The answer is each other.
- This time when you play a few people can help the blindfolded person find their way to the Truth.
- The peoples representing sin will continue to try and block or distract the blindfolded person.
- One or two other people can assist the blindfolded person in searching for truth.

Note: Some of the lessons may take more than one session to complete. It depends on how much discussion there is during the study. I provided a bunch of activities to go along with the lessons. If there is a time when I didi not assign a specific activity, or you need to fill in time to allow a group to finish the discussion, feel free to pick from any activity that has already been completed.

Walking

<u>Focus:</u> Walking, it is part of life. Typically, We go through our day walking along our own path, pursuing our own desires. Do we ever stop and take the time to consider how God wants us to walk? In this study, we will look into God's word and discover how He wants us to walk.

Scripture: Genesis 17: 1-9

(Review and summarize verses. Talk about who Abraham is.)

1. What is God's plan in Abraham? Explain what a covenant is and look up the definition, if needed.

2. Are we descendants of the everlasting covenant? (Remember what we talked about during the Love lesson). If so, what are we asked to do? Hint verse 9.

3. Name the things listed in the passage that we are supposed to do if we want to stay in covenant with God? What promise do we need to remember? Verse 7.

4. God instructed Abraham to walk before him and be blameless. How does God help us to be blameless? (Hint verse 1, what does God do for us.)

5. What can we do to walk with God? (Each member of group shares a thought.)

Scripture: Deuteronomy 11: 22-25 (summarize verses)

6. Describe how God can promise us a nation? (You may have to explain what God means by the term "nation" in context of this verse.)

7. How does this apply to us personally? What are the "nations" that God will drive out of us?

Scripture: Psalm 1: 1-6

8. Compare and contrast the differences between those who choose to delight in the Law and those who choose to walk in the counsel of the wicked.

9. What do the righteous have to stand on? (Explain righteous if needed and look up definition.) Hint verse 6.

Scripture: Matthew 4: 1-11

10. What does Jesus rely on to help him defeat the temptations of the devil?

11. What does knowing God's word enable us to do?

Scripture: 1 John 2: 3-6

12. What is our promise if we walk as Jesus did?

13. What are we if we say that we believe and have faith, but our actions do not line up with our words? Read verse 4 again.

What does it all mean?

14. Describe Gods plan for our lives and what provision does He make for us as we walk with him? Ask each member of your group specifically.

15. This is important. I want to go over it again. How did Jesus overcome the temptations of the devil?

16. How can we walk like Jesus, so that we also can overcome our temptations?

Mining for more: Who is God referring to in Deuteronomy 11:25? Is there any correlation to what we see in our world today? In our society, who is continually being asked to conform? Is the secular society afraid of Christians?

Picturing the Passage

Draw a picture of the nation God promises you.

Activity lesson 3: Walking

In this lesson we focused on our walk with God. The activity for this lesson is something I am calling "The Books of the Bible Rundown." This is a game where teams are tasked with using their knowledge of the books of the Bible to win a race

Materials needed:

- A list of the books of the Bible
- Two volunteers to facilitate the game
- Prize for winning team

Procedure:

- Choose two volunteers
- Volunteer number one will be the "Caller." This person will hold the list of the books of the Bible. This person is responsible for calling out the books of the Bible during the game.
- The second volunteer will be the "Before or After" person. This person is responsible for yelling out the words before or after. This person will yell out the words "Before or After" following the Caller who calls out a book of the Bible. I will explain more in a second.
- Place those who are participating in the Bible Study into groups. The family groups are fine, unless there are obvious inconsistencies in the size of the groups. Then you can adjust the groupings to make the sizes equal.
- You will need to have a starting line and a finish line.

- You will also have to designate how far each group can move ahead if they get a correct answer. What I mean is, you will have to mark spaces from the start to the finish. You can use paper plates, rubber squares, cones, tape, paper, or any other item that will allow all teams to move ahead a standard space.

- When you are ready to begin the game, line up the teams at the starting line.

- The caller yells out a book of the Bible. Any book the caller chooses.

- After the book is yelled out, the before or after person, yells out just that: **before or after**.

- Both the Caller and the "Before and After" person need to listen for the team that calls out the answer first.

- Teams are to call out the answer to whatever the Caller and "Before and After" person yelled out.

- Example: Caller yells: Exodus
    o Before or after person yells out: After
    o Groups need to yell out: Leviticus for a correct answer.

- First team to yell correct answer gets to move ahead one space

- Continue this procedure, calling out different books of the Bible until there is a team that makes it to the finish line.

- Give winning team a prize, play again if there is time.

List of the Books of the Bible

Genesis

Exodus

Leviticus

Numbers

Deuteronomy

Joshua

Judges

Ruth

1 Samuel

2 Samuel

1 Kings

2 Kings

1 Chronicles

2 Chronicles

Ezra

Nehemiah

Esther

Job

Psalms

Proverbs

Ecclesiastes

Song of Solomon

Isaiah

Jeremiah

Lamentations

Ezekiel

Daniel

Hosea

Joel

Amos

Obadiah

Jonah

Micah

Nahum

Habakkuk

Zephaniah

Haggai

Zechariah

Malachi

Matthew

Mark

Luke

John

Acts

Romans

1 Corinthians

2 Corinthians

Galatians

Ephesians

Philippians

Colossians

1 Thessalonians

2 Thessalonians

1 Timothy

2 Timothy

Titus

Philemon

Hebrews

James

1 Peter

2 Peter

1 John

2 John

3 John

Jude

Revelation

Home

Focus: In the beginning, God created Adam and Eve. He took care of them and He blessed them. He walked with them and He gave them a home. When He was finished, He looked at His creation and He said that it was very good. Our homes look strikingly different today compared to what was originally intended. We need to remember what God wants for our homes no matter what they may look like. In this study, we will examine God's plan for our homes.

God's plan

Scripture: Genesis 2:8-10, Genesis 2: 15- 17 (summarize verses)

1. What was the home like that God wanted Adam to have?

2. What was Adam supposed to do in the garden?

Scripture: Genesis 3:1-6

3. Think back to what God told Adam to do in chapter 2, verse 15.

4. Does it sound like Adam was doing his job in chapter 3?

5. What was Adam allowing to happen?

God Provided:

Scripture: Exodus 13:21-22; Exodus 16: 4; Exodus 17: 5-6

6. Describe the home that God provided for the Israelites? Why a cloud and a pillar of fire? What did the cloud do for them during the day, and what did the fire provide at night?

7. What kind of home did God give them?

8. God provided shelter, food, and water for His people in the desert. Are you one of God's people, if so, how does God provide for you?

God Wants:

Scripture: Deuteronomy 6: 4-9 (remember to summarize)

9. What does God want for our homes?

10. What should we fill our homes with? What does God want us to do in our homes?

11. Why does God want us to do this?

12. Why does God love us?

13. What is our spiritual home supposed to look like?

14. Why does God tell us to do so many things to remind us about His love for us?

Scripture: Deuteronomy 6: 20 -25

15. Talk about your personal enslavement in "Egypt." What did God deliver you from? What can God deliver you from?

(Parents tell your children what God did for you to get you to the place that you are at now in your Faith, within reason of course)

(Kids can talk about what distracts them from God. What happens at school or at home that makes us forget about God)

16. Why does God want to deliver us from these things?

(Hint: verses 24 and 25.)

God Will

Scripture: Luke 15: 1-7

17. In this parable, whom does the shepherd represent?

18. Who are the lost sheep?

19. It says that when the shepherd found His lost sheep, He picked it up and He put it on His shoulder. What does it tell us about the shepherd's character?

20. What is God willing to do to get us home?

Scripture: John 3:16

READ TO GROUP: The Shepherd did come for us. The Shepherd did take the sins of the lost sheep upon his back. The Shepherd suffered so that we could know the way that leads to home.

Our Job

Scripture: John 14:23

21. Describe how we invite God into our homes.

22. How can we show God that we love Him?

What does it all mean?

23. Just like Adam, what does God want us to do with the home that he has provided?

24. If we neglect our job, what will happen?

25. What is the most important thing in a home?

26. List steps that you can take to make God the center of your home: (Go back and look through the scripture that we read. Write down the things that God tells us to do, so that you remember them.)

Mining for more: The church should be the Body, the dwelling place, the home for Christ. Does the church reflect the calling described by Peter in 1 Peter 2: 11-12? What is the church called to do in verse 12?

Picturing the Passage

Draw a picture of God's home.

Activity Lesson 4: Home

This lesson focused on making God a priority in our homes on a routine basis. He should be the center of attention daily on our walk through life. This activity will help us to consciously invite God into our homes.

Materials Needed:

- Paper of various colors
- Markers, colored pencils, or anything else that can be collected to be used as decorations.

Procedure:

- Groups will work together to make a card inviting God into their homes. Each family group should make one. If there are single people present, they should also make a card for their own household.
- Groups needs to decorate the invitation.

Groups need to include specific things that they will do in order to make their homes hospitable for God. If we invite a human guest, we go out of our way to make that guest feel comfortable. We should be more than willing to do the same with God. How will you show God hospitality.

Marriage

<u>Focus:</u> God commanded that there be light, and there was light. God commanded that the Earth produce vegetation and He commanded that there be living creatures that fill the expanse of the land, sea, and sky. He looked upon his creation and he said that it was good. God created man, and in the image of God he created them both male and female. He looked upon his creation and He said it was very good!

Unfortunately, in our so-called 'enlightened' culture God's commands hold little water. We call it *'**our responsibility** '* as finite, fallible humans to create, recreate, define and redefine. **We decide to call things very good.** Marriage is one of those God ordained privileges that we have been working at recreating. In this study we will discover the true design for marriage written plainly in God's word.

Scripture: Genesis 1: 27- 28 (remember to summarize the verses)

1. In whose image have we been created?

2. What does it mean to be created in the image of God?

3. Did God place distinctions on the genders that he created?

4. Describe, if you can, how the world is trying to deface the image in which we have been created? What are we hearing in our culture about our own personal choices?

5. How did God bless them? Be careful the answer is implied, it is **not** found after the word and. Hint: it is in the title of this lesson

READ TO GROUP: In the very first chapter of our Bible, God describes His plan for us and for His creation. He created us for a purpose and he wasted no time in telling us what that purpose is.

Scripture: Matthew 19: 4-5

6. Who does Jesus confirm as the author of marriage?

7. When did the arrangement of marriage start?

8. In this passage, who are the two joined "as one flesh"?

9. Who has the authority to join "the two into one"?

10. Who has the authority to change this plan?

Scripture: Genesis 2:18- 25

11. What was God's purpose for creating this first union of man and woman?

12. Did God's purpose for marriage ever change?

13. Even in the exposed state that Adam and Eve were in at the end of this reading, it states that they felt no shame. Why did they feel no shame?

14. If Adam and Eve did feel shame, whom would they be ashamed in front of? Hint: Who was with them in the garden?

15. Do we ever feel ashamed in front of God, be honest? Explain your answer.

16. If you have felt ashamed, what was the cause of the feeling?

17. In this original picture of marriage, we see man and woman standing, shameless before an almighty God. If this is the model for a God centered marriage, what should married couples strive for?

Scripture: Hebrews 13: 4 (This one will be difficult for small children to comprehend. Read the verse and discuss as best as you can. I have written an alternative question below.)

<u>READ TO GROUP:</u> In this verse, we are reminded how to maintain healthy marriages. Parents, if you feel comfortable talking with your children about what God is saying in this verse, please talk freely with them. There are topics in the Bible that are difficult to talk about especially with our children, but that does not mean that we should avoid them. Our culture is continually encouraging us to embrace choices that serve only the gratification of the self. We are told do what feels right to us no matter the consequences. As parents, it is our job to teach our children that there is an order to God's creation. When we abide in that order, God will bless us. When we try to alter that plan of God there is a punishment.

READ TO GROUP: Woe to the obstinate children, declares the LORD, to those who carry out plans that are not mine, forming an alliance, but not by my Spirit, heaping sin upon sin...(*Isaiah 30:1*)

Do your best with this one. Groups with small children can talk about how we can honor God in our relationships with other people.

18. How can we honor God with our actions as we interact with, parents, siblings, friends, etc...?

19. Describe the type of marriage that should be honored by all?

20. How can we keep our marriage bed pure?

21. How can this apply to those who are single or unmarried?

So far, we can see that God is very serious and clear about His design and will for marriage. In the following passages, we will see **<u>why</u>** God is so clear in His presentation of marriage.

Scripture: Matthew 9: 15

22. Who is the bridegroom?

Scripture: John 3: 29

23. Who is the bridegroom? Hint: same as last question.

24. In this verse, John the Baptist is talking. It says that he is full of joy. Why is he full of joy?

25. Again, who is the bridegroom?

26. What does John the Baptist mean when he says: "That joy is mine, and it is now complete."?

27. Can we experience this same complete joy? If so, how?

28. What do we commonly call a man after he is married? This will help with the next section.

Scripture: Ephesians 5: 22- 33

29. Who does Christ represent? Who does the church represent?

30. What is marriage a model of?

31. When we become Christians we are part of whose flesh?

32. As the body of Christ or the church, how are we supposed to present ourselves to the bridegroom?

33. How does God tell us to cleanse ourselves? Verse 26.

34. Weather married or single, we as Christians are all in a marriage covenant with Christ. How can the church, as the bride of Christ, become radiant?

What does it all mean?

35. Throughout the Bible, from the old to the new testament, Did God's intention for marriage ever change?

36. Is God's purpose for marriage still valid? Why?

37. As Christians, we **ALL** enter into a marriage covenant with Christ. List ways that you can Glorify God through this marriage?

Mining for more:

Scripture: Malachi 2: 10 – 14

In these verses, Malachi is in essence talking about those who break faith with God. Malachi is reiterating that God has ordained an order for how things are to fit together for humanity.

38. What does Malachi mean by saying that "Judah has desecrated the sanctuary the Lord loves by marrying the daughter of a foreign god"? Remember in this context Malachi is talking about the tribe of Judah.

39. In verse 12 it says that the man who breaks faith with God will be punished. It goes on to say that he continues to bring offerings to God (he tries to make it look like he still is a follower of God). In verse 13 it says that God will not pay attention to the man any longer, even though he crying to the Lord. Explain why God will no longer pay attention to or accept the offerings of the man?

40. The man tried to make serving God fit into his own lifestyle. He tried to bend the rules so that it would be easy. What is the penalty for trying to recreate something the Lord has ordained?

41. Are we doing this in our own culture in this day? If so what is the consequence?

Picturing the Passage

Draw a picture of God's church.

Activity Lesson 5: Marriage session 1

We are going to play a version of the newly-wed game since we are talking about marriage. We will learn how well we know each other.

Materials:

- Family newly-wed game questions located on the next page.
- Prizes for winning teams.
- Paper.
- Pens, pencils.

Procedure:

- Choose a person to be the game show host.
- This person will be responsible for asking the contestants questions.
- Each group will pick a person to be the spotlight person.
- The spotlight person will go to another room, with the gameshow host.
- Gameshow host will ask the spotlight people from each group a few questions for the family newly-wed game found on page 54.
- You do not need to ask all of the questions, depending on time constraints. Additionally, you are welcome to add your own questions.
- Spotlight people will record their answers on a sheet of paper.
- After the questions are answered, the host and the spotlight people will return to the whole group.
- The host will address the whole group.

- The host will ask the questions presented to the spotlight people to the whole group.
- Ask questions one at a time.
- The host will give the groups time to guess what the spotlight person said as their answer.
- Groups will yell out their answer to the questions.
- Correct answers earn one point for the group.
- Host then asks the next question and the process repeats until all the questions are asked.
- Winning team gets a prize.
- Repeat the game as many times as desired or according to the time.

Family Newly-Wed Game Questions

Questions for kids:

1. What is your favorite food?

2. What is your least favorite food?

3. What is your favorite subject in school?

4. What do you want to do when you grow up?

5. What is your favorite restaurant?

6. What is the silliest thing you ever did?

Questions for adults:

1. What is the strangest gift you ever received?

2. Where is your favorite vacation spot?

3. What is your hobby?

4. How many pairs of shoes do you own?

5. Name something that you have too much of?

6. What is your favorite thing to cook?

7. When you were younger, what did you want to be when you grew up?

8. If you had to move into a new house but could only take one thing with you, what would it be? (excluding family members.)

Activity Lesson 5: Marriage session 2

Because we are talking about marriage, we are going to write vows.

Materials:

- Materials for making a card similar to the earlier activities

Procedures:

- Each group needs to make sure that they know what vows are. Read the definition of vows as a whole group or individually.

Definition:

Webster's Dictionary: a solemn promise or statement, one by which a person is bound to act.

- Each Group should read the following verses
- Define and clarify verses if needed

Instruct the groups to Read 1 John 4: 7 – 12 as a family.

- Groups will then make a card with verses 10 and 11 written out on the card.
- Groups can make cards individually or as a whole family.

Write down one thing that you can commit to as a family to reciprocate the love that God has shown us.

Children

Focus: Children are a gift from God. Life is a gift from God. It is not simply a chance occurrence. There is an overt fervor from the world to instill upon our children, even us for that matter, that life is just a natural process of biology. The world teaches that life begets life; anything outside of that view is religion and is unnecessary.

As Christians, we are called to believe God. The origin of life in God's book is much different than the origin of life found in a common textbook. Since the Beginning, God has a unique plan for his creation. In this study, we will discover God's intent for children. We will learn about the intended relationship between children and parents, children and Christ. Finally, we will be reminded that as adults we are still children of God.

Children's Responsibilities:

Scripture: Exodus 20: 12

1. God gave the Israelites Ten Commandments on Mount Sinai. This is number five of the ten. Why do you think it is important to honor our mothers and fathers?

2. This commandment also comes with a blessing. What is this blessing?

3. Does it mean that if we keep this command we will be promised a long life here on earth?

The next few verses may help explain the meaning of the blessing attached to God's command of honoring our father and mother.

Scripture: Proverbs 8: 32 – 35

4. Whose ways are we to keep?

5. If we honor our mother and father who will bless us?

6. What is the gift God will give us if we listen to Him? Verse 33.

7. In verse 35 it states: "whoever finds me", what does this phrase mean?

8. What is the blessing for those who find Him?

Read to group: Think back to the verses in Exodus: honor your father and mother so that you may live long in the land the Lord God is giving you. In this case God is referring to the land that was promised to Israel. God is not necessarily promising a long physical life on earth. He is offering to bestow His grace and provision to those who abide in Him.

In the context of the verses in Exodus: If the people of Israel abide in God's commands, He promises them a long life in the Promised Land. In other words, God will extend His grace to them He will protect them. This verse applies to us in that, if we apply God's word to our lives, He will also allow us to live in His provision and grace.

Parent/ Adult Responsibilities:

Scripture: Proverbs 22: 6

9. Who is being addressed in this verse? Is this verse only for parents?

10. Parents or adults are to train children up whose way?

11. Describe how adults (this is all adults, not just parents) can help children to stay on track? (What can adults do?) If you have children in your group, ask them for suggestions also.

12. What is the church supposed to do?

What God's commands provide for us:

Scripture: Proverbs 6: 20- 23

13. What are children supposed to do to remind them to keep the commands and teaching? Verse 20 and 21.

14. If this is what the children are supposed to do what does this imply that adults are doing or have done?

15. Verse 21 talks about binding the commands to our hearts, we could take this verse literally, but I do not think that we have to. What does God mean for us to do in this verse?

16. Describe how God's commands can be a light.

17. Describe the world without the light of God's commands.

18. In verse 23 what is the way of life?

19. How should we apply this verse to our own lives?

20. Why should we apply this verse to our own lives?

God's desire for his children:

Scripture: Matthew 19: 13- 14

21. Why does Jesus allow the children to come to him?

Scripture: Matthew 18: 2- 4

22. Verse 3 states that we need to: "change and become like children", what does this verse mean?

Scripture: Matthew 19: 14

23. What does Jesus mean when He says that "the kingdom of heaven belongs to such as these"?

Scripture: Matthew 18: 4- 7

24. How can we approach Christ in humility (verse 4)? Talk about things that get in the way of our ability or even willingness to do this.

25. Christ's message in Verse 6 is frightfully clear. Is our world guilty of what is being stated?

26. Describe ways that the world entices children to sin. (This question can also be applied to adults, how does the world encourage sin?)

27. Think of ways that we as Christians may cause children to sin. (This means us. We are not talking about the secular world anymore; we are talking about the church.)

28. Who or what is to receive the punishment for causing someone to sin?

Read to group: It sounds like Jesus is extremely serious about sin. We need to be vigilant in teaching our children about sin. We should be talking to them about how to identify sin and how to turn away from temptation. We, as adults, are to be examples of how our children are to live as children of God. I am not just talking about parents. I am talking about the church as well.

Scripture John 1: 12-13

29. Whose name will give **All** of us the right to be called children of God?

30. How do we earn that right?

31. From this passage, whom can we see and know as the true author of life? (Who brings life into this world?)

32. In light of this passage, is abortion a Human right? (Remember John's words in verse 13.)

What does it all mean?

33. What is God's will for children?

34. As adults, what is our responsibility for the children who are in our care?

35. What does it mean to have faith like a child?

Mining for more: Jeremiah 3: 19- 20. In these passages, God is speaking through the prophet Jeremiah. To me these verses are heart wrenching. We get a glimpse into the longing that God has for his children. God wants us to call him Father. So often we find ourselves so wrapped up in ourselves that we neglect to call God anything.

What are things that we hold on to that prevent us from having this type of relationship with God?

Picturing the Passage

Draw a picture of Jesus welcoming His children.

Activity Lesson 6: Children session 1

We are talking about family relationships. We are going to be playing a getting to know you exercise for this activity.

Materials:

- Getting to know you questions that are written below.

Procedures:

- This is an intergenerational activity
- Groups will be mixed together for this activity
- Group members take turns asking each other the questions listed below

1. Favorite thing to do when you were younger.
2. Favorite thing to do now.
3. Name 2 things that have changed since you were children. If you are still a child, name 2 things that have changed since you were really little.
4. Talk about a difficulty you have/ had growing up.
5. How can you work through that difficulty? Adults can give advice to kids.

- After game, gather the whole group together and discuss what we learned.

Lesson 6: Children session 2

Continuing with our theme of building intergenerational relationships we will be playing intergenerational kickball

Materials:

- Kickball
- Bases
- Area to play kickball

Procedure:

- Divide the group into two teams. Older members vs. the younger members.
- This will be a basic game of kickball.
- Adults up to bat first.

Sin and Iniquity

<u>Focus:</u> There is one thing that separates us from God. There is one thing that God cannot and will not tolerate. When God created Adam and Eve, it says that He looked upon His work and He said it was very good. **We were created to be very good in the eyes of the Lord.** But Adam failed God; we fail God. Sin entered God's creation. It is said that because of Adam's sin all people sin. In this study, we will begin to discover how God defines the problem of sin.

God's Definition of Sin:

Scripture: Proverbs 6: 16-19

1. Discuss in you group this list of detestable sins. Take the time to define and clarify each one. Talk about each sin and how they relate to the noun associated with the specific sin. Describe what the sins represent. How do they apply to us? You can skip haughty eyes. We are going to address that more in the next question.

2. I do not know if I ever used the word *haughty.* What does this word mean and why is it a sin? (Use your commentary if needed)

Scripture: Isaiah 59: 2-4

3. What separates us from God?

4. What is iniquity?

READ TO GROUP: Most of the time iniquity gets lumped into the category of sin. Iniquity is sin, but it seems that God defines iniquity slightly different that sin. In the Bible we sometimes see the words iniquity and sin in the same verse of scripture. If the words meant exactly the same thing, there would be no reason to use two different words. There must be a distinction between them. We are going to read a couple of verses that help to define the difference between iniquity and sin. I provided a few verses below. I typed the verses from the New King James Version of our Bible. I did this so that all groups can have common language to base our definition of iniquity upon. The NIV and some other translations the word iniquity often gets translated into the word wickedness, worthlessness, vanity and naughtiness. **Read the following verses to your group. Are there any differences between the word iniquity and sin?**

Exodus 34: 6- 9: "And the Lord passed before him and proclaimed, ' The Lord, the Lord God, merciful and gracious, longsuffering and abounding in goodness and truth, keeping mercy for thousands, forgiving **iniquity** and transgressions and **sin**, by no means clearing the guilty, visiting the iniquity of the fathers upon the children and the children's children to the third and fourth generation.'

So Moses made haste and bowed his head toward the earth, and worshipped. Then he said, ' if now I have found grace in Your sight, O Lord, let my Lord, I pray, go among us, even though we are a stiff-necked people; and pardon our **iniquity** and our **sin**, and take us as Your inheritance.'"

Ezekiel 3: 18-19: "When I say to the wicked, 'You shall surely die,' and you give him no warning, nor speak to warn the wicked from his wicked way, to save his life, that same wicked man shall die in his **iniquity**; but his blood I will require at your hand. Yet, if you warn the wicked, and he does not turn from his wickedness, nor from his wicked way, he shall die in his **iniquity**; but you have delivered your soul."

Psalm 32: 5: "I acknowledged my **sin** in you. And my **iniquity** I have not hidden. I said, 'I will confess my transgressions to the Lord,' and you forgave the **iniquity** of my **sin**."

Read to group: To clarify, it is like saying that sin is a group of reptiles and iniquity is a turtle. All turtles are reptiles, but not all reptiles are turtles. Iniquity is sin, but not all sin is classified as iniquity. The Standard Bible Encyclopedia defines the term iniquity as follows: " not an action, but the character of an action." Sin becomes iniquity when we do not repent of the things that we do that are not pleasing to God. We need to be on guard to not allow our character to become complacent in allowing sin to take up residence in our lives.

God provides a distinction between Sin and Iniquity

Sin: an offense against God. A weakened state of human nature in which the self is estranged from God. (Webster's Dictionary)

Iniquity: crookedness, perverseness, lawlessness, wickedness. Sin with intent. Willingness to embrace a sinful nature. The root of sin.

---

5. What are the things that God lists as sins in verse Isaiah 59: 3?

6. What does God mean when he says our hands are stained with blood, your fingers with guilt?

7. List the four things that God points out to us in verse 4. It sounds like Isaiah is talking about a spirit of iniquity in these verses.

8. In verse 4, the text states: "no one calls for justice." Who are we to call to for justice?

9. Discuss what God could be talking about when He says: "They rely on empty arguments and speak lies."

10. List some empty arguments we rely on in our culture:

Scripture: Jeremiah 16: 10-12 (groups with smaller children can answer the following questions or skip to the questions with the heading: 'groups with smaller children.)

11. Do we follow other gods in our day? If so, how and what are they? Explain your answer to your children.

12. Describe how we behave more wickedly than our fathers as it says in verse 12?

Groups with smaller children: Talk about the ways that our culture perceives sin. Do we really think it is a big deal? How does our culture influence our children, given the fact that we embrace sin in so many ways? What can we do about it as families?

13. What is a stubborn heart?

14. What could be considered "stubborn" in your own heart? (Parents, answer the question for yourself, then talk your children about what it looks like in their own lives.)

Our Sin Nature: Read the following to your group.

Scripture Provided: Isaiah 14: 12- 14, reads: "How you have fallen from heaven, O Lucifer, son of the morning! How you are cut down to the ground, you who weakened the nations! For you have said in your heart: ' I will ascend to heaven, I will exalt my throne above the stars of God; I will also sit on the mount of the congregation on the farthest sides of the north; I will ascend above the heights of the clouds, I will be like the Most High.'"

This passage is taken from the NKJV translation of the Bible. This translation gives a clear account of the events written about in the passage.

15. Where can we conclude that our sin nature originated from as we read this passage?

16. There are a number of things against Gods order that are listed in this passage. Lucifer (Satan) claims that He will bring these claims into being. What is the sin Lucifer committed against God?

Scripture: James 1: 13 – 15

17. Lucifer brought sin to the world when He fell. Where does our individual sin nature come from, vs. 14?

18. Is God the author of sin and temptation?

19. What is the result of allowing sin to thrive in your life?

Scripture: Ecclesiastes 8: 11

20. Why do we continue to sin?

21. Do we see this verse come to life in our world today? Explain.

What does it all mean?

22. God makes His definition of sin very clear. We know when we commit an act of sin because we experience a guilty conscience. God gave us this warning sign so that we do not allow sin to take root in our hearts. Discuss possible consequences for allowing sin to go unchecked. See John 12: 40.

23. God did **NOT** design us to have a sin nature. This aspect of our character makes itself known when we place our own desires first. What can we do to keep our sin nature in control?

We will continue our study of sin in our next lesson. The discussion will revolve around why sin does not go away and God's plan for dealing with the sin problem.

Mining for more:

The "church" as a whole in America is often compared to the church of Laodicea written about in the book of revelation. Read Revelation 3: 14- 17. Compare the church of Laodicea to the modern church in the U.S. What does Christ say he will do if the church does not repent?

Picturing the Passage

Draw a picture of a sinful heart.

Draw a picture of a heart that is full of God's love.

Activity lesson 7: Sin and Iniquity session 1

We will be creating a sin box for the activity. This box will help us to remember to pray and ask God to forgive us of our sins.

Materials:

- Oak tag or cardstock paper
- Cube template.
- Template can be found and printed from online sources.
- Markers and things to decorate box
- Scissors
- Tape

Procedure:

- Each group will get a cube template.
- Have groups trace the template.
- They can decorate the template
- Fold template together to make a box. Use tape to connect the box.
- Write on slips of paper the sins that you struggle with.
- Place the slips of paper in the box.
- This will remind you to pray for those things that you do that are not pleasing to God.
- Remember to ask Him to forgive you of your sins.

Activity Lesson 7: Sin and Iniquity session 2

We will continue to focus our attention on overcoming sin. This activity is called sin dodge ball.

Materials:

- Dodge balls
- Area to play dodgeball

Procedure:

- Ask those who are playing the following question.
- After asking the question explain that sin tries to run around and ruin our lives. The Word of God is the weapon to get rid of sin

ASK TO GROUP: What is one of the weapons to get rid of sin?

- Explanation of game:
- Some players will represent sin
- Two players will be regular people
- One person will represent the Word of God
- The players who represent sin will run around trying to not let the word of God get to the person. They can catch or deflect the ball, trying to prevent the person from being hit by the Word

- The two players who represent people will try to be hit by the Word of God. If they are hit, they get to stand with the Word. They can also get a ball to try get sin out.

- The thrower will be the Holy Spirit. The ball represents the sword, the word of God.

- The thrower will try to throw the ball to the players who represent people.

- Sin can try to catch or deflect the word before it gets to the person. If sin catches or deflects the word nothing happens. If sin gets hit with the word, then sin is out and needs to sit down.

- Game ends when all of sin is destroyed

Lesson Eight

Why We Sin

Focus: Last time we looked at God's definition of sin and the sin nature that we inherited. We will continue our study of sin with this lesson. **We will seek to answer the question: why do we still struggle with sin when we know that we serve an Almighty God?** We will also learn about God's reaction to sin and His plan to rid us of the problem of sin.

These subjects are difficult to talk about. We often try to glaze over them and think only about the nice stuff. Even though we do not like it, a study of sin is essential to know the truth found in the whole council of God. If we know what can bring us down, we will also know what can lift us up.

Our lack of fear

Scripture: Romans 1:20

1. Why are we without excuse?

2. The verse states that we are without excuse because God's invisible qualities have been understood since the beginning. Describe how we know God's invisible qualities?

Read to Group: In the book "Mere Christianity" C.S. Lewis describes this understanding of God in the chapter titled "The Law of Human Nature." He explains that all of humanity has a sense of morality. This moral sensitivity is essentially the same across cultures. We all have an innate understanding of what is right and what is wrong, no matter where you live on this earth. This understanding occurs outside of ourselves. We then, as individuals, have the capacity to choose to follow what is right or what is wrong. But no matter our individual choice, the overarching knowledge of what is right is still there. It exists beyond our choices and how we decide to act on a personal level. I believe that C.S. Lewis is elaborating upon what Paul was talking about in Romans 1:20. We recognize that there is a 'goodness' that transcends any choice that we make. This unchanging 'goodness', this 'moral rightness', is God. We are without excuse because we all know that there is a God who is infinitely good as well as infinitely just.

Scripture: James 4: 14- 17

3. If we are without excuse, why do we choose sin? verse. 16

Scripture: 1 Corinthians 2: 12-14

4. List things that come from the Spirit of God? Talk about verses 12 and 13 say and Galatians 5: 22-23 may also help.

5. Are these things found to be foolishness in our world today? Explain your answer.

Scripture: Ephesians 2:1-3

6. What causes us to be dead in our sins?

7. Why is it so easy to follow our sinful nature?

8. Who is the ruler of the kingdom of the air?

9. Who is he still at work in?

10. As Christians, do we need to allow this ruler to direct our thoughts and actions?

Scripture: Romans 3: 11-12

11. Why are we allowed to live in sin?

12. Why are we allowed to follow our sinful desires?

Scripture: Romans 3:18

13. Describe what is meant by fear of God?

14. Why should we Fear God?

Scripture: John 12: 43

15. What does this say about our sin nature?

16. Why do we not seek praise from God?

Scripture: Psalm 14:1

17. In what part of the body does the fool make the claim that there is no God?

18. Is claiming something in your heart worse than just speaking it? Why?

Scripture: Romans 3:18

19. Describe the kind of fear that we are supposed to have for God.

Read to Group: I believe this verse marks the place on God's timeline where the modern church finds itself in this day. We are at a pivotal point in history when God's true church and the apostate church are beginning to draw apart from each other. God has been calling His true church closer to himself. He is awakening the spirit that is in all true believers to seek Him more completely. While doing this, He is allowing the church of the whitewashed walls, the church filled with half-hearted devotion, to drift toward their own demise.

Paul is explaining in Romans 3 verse 18 the cause for this division. We have come to a place in human history where there is very little reverent respect and fear for our Creator. In the book "The attributes of God," A.W. Tozer writes about God's justice. He states that: "If there is an iniquitous, unequal, unatoned, uncleansed, unprotected sinner in his sin, there is only one answer- all of God says, 'Death and Hell.' And all of heaven can't pull that man up.

But if he beats his breast and says, 'God be merciful to me a sinner' (Luke 18:13), and takes the benefits of the agony of God on a cross, God looks down on that moral situation and says, 'Life!' And all of hell can't drag that man down." Tozer is saying that God has come to suffer the punishment that was due us for our sin. God paid for our salvation through His suffering. If we accept this gift, God looks upon us with mercy. If we choose to not accept that gift, we choose God's judgment of condemnation toward sin. God's judgment of sin is death and suffering.

David Platt describes it this way: **"What we've been saved from, by God's grace, is God Himself."** There will be a day when God will be done with sin and His wrath will be unleashed so that this world falls into order again. God's desire for us is that we all come to know Him, and that none should suffer. So the question that we need to ask ourselves is: "Do I fear God enough to follow him?"

In this last section, we discovered that we continually follow our sin nature. We saw how easy it is to just comply with this nature. This happens because we lift ourselves up and we consider the things of God foolish, at times. We have lost out fear of God. To clarify this fear: we are not supposed to be afraid of Him; we are supposed to revere Him. We are to look to Him with awe and see His greatness. No matter how hard we try, we cannot compare to him.

God's Reaction:

Scripture: Isaiah 3: 10- 11

20. Who are the righteous in verse 10?

22. Who are the wicked in verse 11?

23. What is God's plan for the wicked?

Scripture: Malachi 4: 1- 2

24. Describe what Malachi means when he says "surly the day is coming?" Whose day is it?

25. How does God describe the people in verse 1?

26. Discuss God's plan for people who choose to live in sin.

27. What is the promise to those who revere the name of the Lord?

Scripture: Matthew 10: 32- 34

28. What promise does Jesus make in verse 32?

29. What does Jesus mean when He says that He did not come to bring peace but a sword?

Scripture Revelation 19: 11- 16

30. Who is the rider on the white horse?

31. In these verses, what is Jesus coming to do?

32. It says in the text that out of Jesus' mouth comes a sword. I do not think an actual sword is coming from His mouth. What does this image mean?

33. Does Jesus' plan for sin differ from God's plan? Verse 15.

34.   Read verse 16 again, out loud!

What does it all mean?

35. We discovered that part of our problem with sin is our lack of fear toward God. As a review, talk about what it means to have a reverent fear of God. Does it mean that we are supposed to be afraid of Him?

36. In Psalm 14 the text reads that a fool says in his heart that there is no God. List things that we can do to avoid being a fool.

37. Sin is definitely something that we cannot take lightly. God had a plan to eliminate sin from the beginning. From what we have read, did God's plan for sin ever change?

Mining for more

Read Matthew 10: 34- 39. Jesus is talking about some serious stuff in these verses.

Does He mean what He says?

Why does Jesus state that He may turn a man against his father or a daughter against her mother?

If we are followers of Christ, we are called to take up our own cross. Christ's cross was salvation. What is your cross?

Picturing the Passage

Draw a picture of Jesus coming as King ofKings and
Lord of Lords!

Activity lesson 8

We will play a game to help us understand how difficult it is to get rid of sin in our lives.

Materials:

- 25 sheets of recycled paper
- tape

Procedure:

- Divide groups into two teams
- Crumble up all 25 sheets of paper
- Have one group sit on one side of the room and the other group sit on the opposite side.
- Place a strip of tape down the middle of the room to divide the room in half
- Explain that the crumbled paper will represent sin
- Each group will have 4 or 5 minutes to try and throw all of the sin onto the other groups side of the room
- Place the paper into the playing area
- Give groups time to get rid of their sin

After time is up explain that it is impossible to try to get rid of sin on our own. Discuss how we are to deal with sin.

The Problem of Sin

Focus: Sin is when we do something against the will of our God. We know when we sin because we can feel it in our hearts. It is said that God wrote His laws into our hearts. When we break them He lets us know.

Sin is the one thing that has the power to separate us from God forever. God knows this, and He also knows that we are weak. We make a lot of mistakes. Throughout our Bible, God tells us His plan to eliminate the power sin has over our lives. In this lesson, we will discuss God's solution for the problem of sin.

Scripture: Genesis 3:13-15 (summarize verse)

1. What is Enmity? (Look up the word, if you need to).

2. Who is God putting enmity between?

3. There are two groups of offspring in this verse, who is the offspring of the woman (Eve)?

4. Describe the other group of offspring in this passage, who are they from?

5. What is the difference between the two groups?

READ TO GROUP: From the beginning, God had a plan for the problem of sin. We will now read through just a few of the prophesies in the Old Testament that foretold the coming of the one who crushes the serpents head.

Scripture: Isaiah 7:14

6. Who fulfilled this prophecy?

7. What does Immanuel mean? How did Jesus fulfill this?

Scripture: Micah 5:2

8. Where does the ruler who is being spoken about in this verse come out of?

9. Who fulfilled this prophecy?

10. Even though Micah is talking about a future ruler for Israel, he states that the ruler will be "of old, from ancient times." How can a future ruler also be from ancient times?

Scripture: Isaiah 61: 1-2 (remember to summarize)

11. Who is being spoken about in this verse?

Scripture: Luke 4:14-21

12. Who said that he fulfilled the prophecy written about in Isaiah?

13. How can Jesus have the authority to say such things?

14. Jesus says that He came to proclaim freedom for the prisoners and recovery of sight for the blind, to release the oppressed, who is Jesus talking about in this verse?

15. What causes us to be prisoners?

16. Christ did heal the blind, but in this verse, I think He is also talking about us. In our world what can cause us to be blind?

Scripture: Zechariah 9:9

17. Who is the King being described in this verse?

18. What event is recorded in the New Testament that happened seven days after the fulfillment of this prophesy?

Scripture: Zechariah 9:9

19. What event is recorded in the New Testament that happened   seven days after the fulfillment of this prophesy?

Scripture: Zechariah 13: 7

20. Who is the shepherd that has been struck?

21. Discuss the reason why the shepherd needed to be struck.

22. In this passage, God states "Awake, O sword, against my shepherd, against the man who is close to me!" What is compared to a sword elsewhere in our Bible? (Ephesians 6:17 may help.)

23. Name the weapon that came against the shepherd.

24. Who was in charge of carrying this verse out?

READ TO GROUP: This is a tough verse. I believe that it is in our Bible to remind us that even in the most tragic events, God is in control. We were once sinners, condemned to suffer God's wrath. But we know that God had a plan for us since the beginning. We read in Genesis, that God said He would provide a Savior. Nothing would get in the way of God fulfilling His promise. This verse in Zechariah shows us that God's word can be trusted and it will never change. He will keep His promises to us no matter what.

Scripture: Isaiah 53: 2- 5

25. Again, whom is this verse referring to?

26. What does Isaiah mean when he says "He had no beauty or majesty to attract us to him, nothing in his appearance that we should desire him."

27. In lesson number seven we defined the difference between sin and iniquity. Isaiah writes in verse 5 that "he was crushed for our iniquities", describe what Isaiah means in this verse.

Scripture: Psalm 22: 14- 18

28. What is this passage describing?

Read to Group: This Psalm is thought to have been written approximately 700 years before Jesus was born, yet it is written almost as if Jesus himself were speaking it as He hung on the cross. The Persians are said to be the inventors of crucifixion. It is believed that they started using it as a form of capital punishment around 90 B.C. This Psalm, which describes the agony of crucifixion, was written hundreds of years before anyone knew what crucifixion even was. God is good. His word is true. God will keep his word. We can be assured that HE is and forever will be our Savior.

Scripture: Psalm 22: 7-8

29. In verse 7, whom are they mocking?

30. In verse 8, whom are they mocking? **(Think about this one)**

Scripture: Psalm 22: 1

Scripture: Matthew 27:46

READ TO GROUP: "Awake, O Sword, against my shepherd, against the man who is close to me!"

Jesus suffered the punishment that we were due. Jesus drank the cup of God's wrath for us. He suffered the agony of crucifixion unto death and he paid the penalty of our sin. But worst of all, at this point in

history, Jesus was condemned to separation from God. This is also our fate if we do not accept the gift of Christ. Fortunately, we know the rest of the word. Three days later Christ rose from the dead and 40 days after that He ascended to heaven to be reunited with the Father. Because of these victorious events, we have the full assurance that God will and does provide.

What does it all mean?

31. What was God's plan to save us from sin all the way at the beginning of our Bible? Did God's plan ever change? Can we count on God to keep His word?

32. It seems clear to me that there is only one way to be saved from our sin. Who can we count on to pay that price?

33. What does it mean when we say that Jesus paid the price?

Mining for more:

Read 2 Peter 1: 16- 21. Where does the word of prophecy come from?

34. How can prophecy be a "light shining in a dark place"?

Jesus often spoke with great authority when talking with His followers. In this passage, Peter is also speaking with great authority. How can Peter speak with such staunch authority?

Picturing the Passage

Draw a picture of a Sword that represents the Word of God.

Activity lesson 9

The Word of God is the Sword that will destroy sin in our lives. It is essential that we rely on the accomplishment of Jesus on the Cross. He is the only Truth that can set us free form sin.

Materials:

- Various papers to make a sword
- Scissors
- Glue
- Markers

Procedure:

- Draw the shape of a sword on a sheet of paper. You can use pictures or the internet for reference
- Cut out the sword
- Write the Bible verse on the sword. Bible verse Hebrews 4:12.
- Decorate the sword if you wish

The Son of Man

Focus: The Son of Man is a strange term. It is a title that Jesus calls Himself numerous times throughout the New Testament. This term was first used in the book of Daniel. In this book, Daniel was given a vision from God about the ONE who will be given authority and sovereign power to rule, eternally, over all nations and languages. Daniel refers to this individual as the son of man. When Jesus calls himself the Son of Man, He is declaring that He is the One who Daniel was writing about. In this study we will discuss why the Son of man came and what He commands us to do as His followers.

Scripture: Isaiah 9: 2- 7 (summarize verse)

1. Who was born? Who was He born for?

2. Who gave Him?

3. Why was he given? Verses 5- 7 will help.

4. In verse 2, it states that those people who were walking in darkness have seen a light and that a light has dawned for those living in the land of the shadow of death. What is this great light that has been shown to them?

5. Why was their joy increased? The answer may be in verse 4.

6. Verse 7 ends with the sentence "The zeal of the Lord Almighty will accomplish this." Who is the one that possesses such unyielding zeal for God the Father?

7. Why will all those things listed in this passage come to pass?

Scripture: Luke 2: 1- 7

8. Why did Joseph and Mary need to go to Bethlehem?

9. Whose ancestral line did Joseph belong to?

10. Who and what was David?

Scripture: Isaiah 9:7

11. Who will reign on David's throne?

Read to Group: Jewish tradition sometimes refers to the Messiah as having two personifications or incarnations. One incarnation is called Meshiach ben Yosef (Messiah as son of Joseph.) Joseph being the one with the fancy colored coat. This is how Jesus came to earth the first time. He came as the suffering servant. He came **first** to restore us unto God the Father. During this first advent of the Messiah, the nation of Israel was looking for a different kind of Redeemer.

The other incarnation of the Messiah, according to Jewish tradition, is called Meshiach ben David (Messiah as son of David.) This advent of the Messiah is called the conquering king. This is the Messiah that Israel **was** looking for when Jesus walked among them.

In Luke chapter two, we read that Joseph and Mary needed to go to Bethlehem, the town of David, because Joseph belonged to the house of King David. Luke put this in his writing to point to the fact that Jesus will be born into the family line of David. Jesus will one day return as the long awaited

Messiah be David, the conquering King. He will sit on the throne of David and take possession of this lost world.

Scripture Daniel 7:14

12. Describe the kingdom that Christ will have dominion over.

13. What is meant by the phrase "men of every language worshipped him?"

14. Describe what His dominion will be like.

Scripture: Luke 2: 8-14

15. Who testified that Jesus is Savior?

16. How many angels?

17. How can we find peace on Earth? Verse 14.

18. Talk about how we can find favor with God?

Scripture: Luke 2: 15- 20 (remember to summarize)

19. What did the shepherds do when they saw Jesus? Verse 17.

20. What should we do with the knowledge of our Savior Jesus Christ?

21. How are we to respond to God's word? (Verse 20)

Scripture: Matthew 4: 18- 22

22. What were they doing when Jesus called them?

23. Jesus came to Peter and the others while they were in the middle of their everyday routine. Jesus told them to put down their nets (everyday routine) and follow Him. In the routine of our day, what are we called to do?

24. How can we follow Christ in our everyday? Be specific, name things that you can do and are willing to do every day. Ask the children what they can do while in school or with friends.

Scripture: Matthew 16: 24-27

25. How do we deny ourselves?

26. When we deny ourselves from something, we often feel like it is a burden, a hardship or a chore to complete. In our Christian walk, is this how we should feel in light of this verse?

27. Who are we doing the "denying of ourselves" for?

28. Jesus tells us to sacrifice the things in our lives that could distract us from drawing closer to Him. Is Jesus right in telling us to do this? Why or why not?

29. If we feel like it is a chore to make sacrifices in our everyday lives, who or what needs to change?

30. Discuss what Jesus is talking about in verse 25?

31. How can we save our lives by losing them?

32. Discuss how we can gain the whole world but forfeit the soul?

33. What is better the world or the soul?

34. How will we be rewarded if we choose wisely?

35. Verse 27 states that we will be "rewarded for what we have done." This is not talking about earning our reward, what does Jesus mean in this verse? What have we done?

Scripture: John 10: 27- 30

36. Who are Christ's sheep?

37. What does Jesus give His sheep?

38. If we continue to follow Jesus, who can snatch us out of His hand?

39. Can we rely on this to be true? If so, how do we know?

Scripture: Matthew 19: 28-29

40. Where does Jesus state that He will sit?

41. Why did Jesus come? Verse 28.

What does it all mean?

42. Because He was given by an infinite God, **because He came** what are we to do?

43. When we choose to follow Jesus whom are we following? Think about His human family tree? Who orchestrated all of these events to fit together so perfectly?

44. What does Christ want us to do in order to make Him the light in our lives?

45. What can we do if following Christ feels like a chore or a burden in our lives?

46. What are some practical things that you can do in your everyday to tell others about the love of Jesus?

Mining for more:

Read Daniel 7: 13-14. Who is talking in these verses?

47. We know who the Son of Man is, but who is the Ancient of Days?

48. Who was given authority?

49. Who will worship Him?

50. Has this event happened yet?

51. Now go back to the verse in Matthew, chapter 16: 27. How will Jesus come?

52. Now turn to Revelation 19: 11- 16. Who is being described in these verses?

53. What is written on His thigh?

54. How is the church preparing for the return of this coming KING?

Picturing the Passage

Draw a picture of Jesus as King!

Activity lesson 10

Jesus is our King. He needs to have a special place in our hearts. We will make a visual reminder of His place of prominence.

Materials:

- Red construction paper
- Gold or yellow construction paper
- Markers
- Scissors

Procedures:

- Draw the shape of a heart on a paper
- Cut out heart
- Draw the shape of the Ark of the Covenant on the Gold or yellow paper
- Cut out Ark
- Glue God's throne onto the heart
- Write John 18:37 and Revelation 17:4 on the heart

Lesson Eleven

Sheep

Focus: John 10:14 says: "My sheep listen to my voice; I know them, and they follow me."

In this verse Jesus is talking about a personal relationship. He is talking about the relationship that we as Christians have with the One True Shepherd. This Shepherd will stop at nothing to ensure that His sheep are safe and that they are with Him.

We know that the Shepherd will be diligent in keeping His Word, the problem is with the sheep. We as sheep have a tendency to wonder, sometimes even forgetting that we are sheep. In this study, we will discover what our job is as followers of Christ.

Scripture: Matthew 28: 18- 20 (summarize verse)

1. What authority does Jesus have? Who gave Him the authority?

2. In this passage what command does Jesus give us?

3. Discuss what it means to make a disciple?

4. In verse 20, Jesus tells us to teach. What does a teacher need to do in order to be able to teach?

5. A teacher must first know to be able to teach. Discuss what we need to do in order to be able to teach?

Read to Group: Knowing that this is the command that Jesus gives us, how do we follow Christ? (Don't answer this now)

Scripture: Matthew 22: 34-40

6. What does it mean to love God with all your heart?

7. What does it mean to love God with all your soul?

8. Answer the same question but replace heart and soul with mind?

9. Jesus added to the first of the Ten Commandments by stating love your neighbor as yourself. First, who is your neighbor? Second, How do we love them as ourselves?

Read to Group: In the book "The Weight of Glory", C.S. Lewis comments on what we are in the eyes of God. Lewis talks about how we interact with other people, our neighbors. He comments on the fact that we all have a relationship with eternity. Lewis is quoted as saying: "There are no *ordinary* people. You have never talked to a mere mortal, Nations, cultures, arts, civilizations- these are mortal, and their life is to ours as the life of a gnat. But it is immortals whom we joke with, work with, marry, snub, and exploit-immortal horrors or everlasting splendors."

What Lewis is saying is that, we are all immortal spirits. We dwell in a fallen state currently in this temporal body, but our souls are forever. They are forever no matter if we accept the precious gift of the shed blood of Christ or not. If we accept Christ, God sees us as everlasting splendors. If we reject Christ, we are immortal horrors.

Lewis goes on to encourage us, in the book, to remember this as we come into contact with those people whom Christ calls our neighbors. We need to understand that we are all immortal- everlasting splendors in the eyes of God, or immortal horrors. Our job is to express God's love to those around us. We need to be an encouragement to the splendors and hope and conviction for the horrors.

10. Summarize what we are commanded to do in order to follow Christ.

Scripture: John 13:34- 35

11. What is the new command that Jesus gives us? (Be careful not to just stop after the first sentence, who modeled this love?)

12. What is the result of loving one another? Verse 35.

Read to group: God gave the nation of Israel commands (613 of them) on how to dress and how to live, even what to eat. God did this because He wanted His chosen people to be set apart, to look different than the rest of the world. God wanted them to be a witness to the people around them and to show others God's love by the way that they lived.

Most Christians, including ourselves, look pretty much the same as everyone else. We do not dress or even act any differently than the average person walking down the street. But in the passage that we just read, Jesus declares that we should be known by our love. This is the thing that should set us apart from the rest of the world.

13. How could something like love be enough to set us apart from the rest of the world in our day?

14. How can we live a life that is an example of Christ's love?

Scripture: 1 Peter 4:10

15. Discuss what we are to do in verse 10.

16. If we are able to do this, what are we an example of?

17. Are we to serve others in order to ultimately make ourselves feel good?

18. When we serve others, who should be praised?

Scripture: 1 John 3:16

(If you have younger people in your group, you may need to explain what is meant by the use of the word brothers in this context.)

19. What does it mean to lay down our lives for our brothers?

Scripture: 1 John 3: 17- 20

20. Why is it not enough to love with just our words?

21. In verse 19, what is the truth?

22. How can we know that we belong to the truth?

23. Does this mean that we need to live perfect lives in order to be with God?

24. Read verse 20 again. Who is greater than all the mistakes that we will ever make?

25. Who knows that we have made and will continue to make countless mistakes in our lives?

26. How can we restore our relationship to God after we sin?

Scripture: James 2: 14- 17

27. I will rephrase a question from the section that we just read in 1 John. Why is it not enough to claim to have faith with just our words?

Read to Group: We can say a whole bunch of stuff and not really mean it. As they say, the proof is in the pudding, our words should be a reflection of our lives. If the image in the mirror does not match the image that we speak about when we talk about ourselves, there is something wrong.

28. Do you agree with the statement that James makes in verse 17?

29. What are the works that our faith should produce?

Scripture: Philippians 2: 12- 13

30. What does Paul mean when he says " continue to work out your faith with fear and trembling"?

31. Who works within us? Whose purpose is being worked out?

32. As Christians, should we seek ways that we can work to build up God's kingdom?

Scripture: 1 Peter 4: 1-2

33. What is the attitude that we are to have?

34. What does it mean to suffer in the body? Does this mean that we have to torture or torment ourselves?

35. If we intentionally deny our human desires, what will we be done with?

36. What should we seek to live the rest of our lives for?

37. Why should we do this?

What does it all mean?

38. The end of Matthew chapter 28 is called the Great Commission. Jesus tells us to go out and teach the Word of God and make disciples. How can we do this?

Think about what we read in the books of 1 John and James.

39. Why should we love one another?

40. As Christians, should we seek out opportunities to "work out our Faith?"

41. How can you practically apply this to your life? What can you do to "work out your faith?"

Mining for more:

One thing that Satan will throw at the Sheep is doubt. Satan wants us to doubt our faith because our faith is what protects us and guides us until Christ returns.

We can read about doubt when God himself was hovering above the Israelites in the desert. We read about doubt among the anointed kings of the Jewish nation. We can read about doubt even among the disciples that walked with Christ.

Read: Matthew 17: 1-7, and then Matthew 28: 16-17.

In these verses, even after a supernatural vision and a confirmation by God, some of the disciples had doubt. They doubted because they were not yet living by faith. They were still looking for the Messiah ben David. They were looking for the conquering king.

Read Acts1: 13- 14, Acts 2: 1-6, Acts 2: 42- 47.

In these verses, we can see the origin of the New Testament church. We read, in the book of Acts, about those who believed based on the faith that was set into their hearts. We as the "modern" church are also to live by the same faith. In the book of John, Jesus gives us a beautiful confirmation of the blessing that comes through faith.

Read John 20:29

We are those who have not seen yet have believed. Because of Christ's love for us, because we believe, we have been given this precious gift of faith. We know because we have not seen. The recognition and salvation of Almighty God dwells within us through faith. What power faith possesses.

42. How can we bolster our faith, when doubt of our Creator arises?

Read in Closing: 1 Peter 1: 3-9

Picturing the Passage

Draw a picture of yourself as a sheep.!

Activity lesson 11

God promises us that His sheep hear His voice. The world makes it difficult to hear the voice of God. There are so many distractions. We are going to play a game that will illustrate the difficulty that we have in hearing God's voice.

Materials:

- Paper with a Bible verse written on it. Keep the verse short.
- Stuff that the group can make noise with ex. Instruments, sticks etc...

Procedure:

- Select a few people from the large group to be the noise makers. Two or three should be plenty. If the group is very large, more noisemakers can be chosen
- Have group sit in a circle. The noise makers will stay to the side.
- Explain that we will be playing the whisper down the lane game. We will be reciting a Bible Verse to the person sitting to our right. We are to whisper the verse into the persons ear. They are then to whisper the same verse into the ear of the next person. Continue until the group comes full circle.
- Last person in circle recite what was whispered into their ear
- While the group is whispering, the noisemakers will be making noise and trying to distract the group.
- Talk about why it was difficult to whisper the correct answer all the way down the group.
- Talk about why it is difficult to hear the voice of God

- Try the game again. This time give the first person in line the paper with the Bible verse written on it.
- This time the group members can read the verse as they whisper in their neighbor's ear.
- Pass the Bible verse around the group.
- Noisemakers will be making noise in an attempt to distract the group
- When the message comes full circle, recite the final answer
- Talk about why it was easier to complete the task this time.
- Ask group where we can find the instructions of God written down so that we do not get confused.

The Power of Faith

Focus: As believers, children of Almighty God we are faced with numerous challenges. We live in a fallen world and this world is becoming increasingly hostile toward all the things of God. But, though we will have challenges, God does not leave us without hope. He gives us the power found in faith to conquer all that might try to deceive us.

Scripture: Exodus 17: 8- 13 (review and summarize verses. Restate the verse in your own words to help everyone to understand what God is saying.)

1. Who did Moses have faith in?

2. Is there any evidence in this passage that Moses doubted the provision of God?

3. Who did Moses give honor to by acting this way? (Hint: where were his hands pointing?)

4. What was/were the limitations of Moses' faith? (Hint: think about the beginning of verse 12.)

5. Discuss the things that hinder our own faith.

6. Who did Moses rely on for support? Who can we rely on?

7. When we walk in faith, should we expect immediate answers? (end of verse 12.)

8. What is our part in the power of faith?

Scripture: Joshua 6: 1-9 (remember to summarize verse.)

9. Why was Jericho shut up?

10. Why was the city closed up because of Israel? (Hint: think about the reputation that preceded Israel.)

11. As Christians, are we supposed to strike fear (at least respect for God's name) to the world around us? Are we supposed to have a reputation like the one that followed Israel?

12. How can we get the secular world to *shut up*? Is this something that is still possible?

13. What were Joshua and the Israelite army asked to demonstrate in vs. 3-4?

(Hint: it was not a show of strength as a way to intimidate the people of Jericho.)

Scripture Joshua 6: 12-16

14. If we have faith, where does that faith come from?

15. Why did the Israelite army have such faith in God?

16. Does God do anything in your life to solidify your faith?

Scripture: Joshua 6:20

<u>Read to Group:</u> We are born into a fallen world. We have inherited a sin nature. When we are born we are given a body that is similar to the city of Jericho, tightly shut up. We close ourselves off to God because of sin. It takes a step of faith to open us up.

17. What cause the walls of the city to collapse? The answer is in one sense God, but I think there is also another answer to this question.

18. What are the walls of your life that the power of faith had to break through? Are there any walls that still need to be broken down?

19. What are you willing to do to allow God to dwell in your city?

Scripture: 1 Samuel 17: 31-37

20. Who did David have faith in?

21. Where did David's confidence come from?

22. Why was David motivated to fight Goliath? (hint verse 37)

23. Who would deliver David through this trial?

Scripture: 1 Samuel 17: 41- 47

24. In whose name did David come to the battle in?

25. What does the name Lord of Hosts mean?

26. What did David claim would be the result of the battle? (hint verses 46- 47)

Scripture: 1 Samuel 17: 48- 49

27. How did David approach Goliath? Did he hide and try to ambush him?

28. Who was the source of power for David's faith?

29. When we experience trials or difficulties in our lives, who should we rely on to deliver us?

30. How do we seek God 's help in times of difficulty?

READ TO GROUP: Though we do not have a giant to fight like Goliath, we are in a battle, just like David. Our battle is a spiritual battle. The giant of our world wants to destroy our soul. Our enemy wants to deceive us so that we do know recognize God. our enemy wants to confuse us so much so that we do not recognize the source of our Salvation. We can have confidence in God that He will deliver us through any difficulty. He is the only hope that we have to overcome the battles that we face in our lives.

Scripture: 2 Corinthians 10: 3- 6

31. What is the nature of the battle that we face?

32. What does it mean when Paul writes that we do not walk in the flesh?

33. Who and what are we at war with?

34. What type of weapons do we fight with? (hint verse 4)

35. What empowers those weapons?

36. What are we to do in this war?

Our response in the power of our faith: How we find victory in the battle.

Scripture: Deuteronomy 10:12- 13

37. List the commands God gave us in these verses.

38. Name some things in your group that can show God that you love Him? (Each member of the group needs to list at least one.)

Scripture: Deuteronomy 30: 15- 19

39. What are the two choices?

40. What is required if we choose life?

41. What are the consequences if we do not obey God?

42. How can we be drawn away and worship other gods in our lives today?

Scripture: Matthew 6:33

43. What are we supposed to seek first?

44. How do we seek His Kingdom?

45. How do we seek His righteousness? (You may have to discuss what righteousness is with the younger members of your group.)

46. For the sake of time, I only included verse 33 in the last scripture reference. In context of the chapter, Jesus is talking about how to be an obedient follower. He says that if we seek God's Kingdom "all these things will be added to" us. Quickly summarize what He means by this statement. (You may have to skim through the chapter.)

Scripture: Titus 3: 4-7

47. How are we justified?

48. What is the result of placing our faith in the Salvation of Jesus Christ?

What does it all mean?

49. We read about Moses, Joshua and David in this study, who did all of those people put their faith in? Who are we to put our faith in?

50. Review some of the results of placing our faith in God.

51. Why is it important to obey God?

52. If we obey God what will He help us have victory over?

Mining for more:

Deuteronomy 32: 15-18:

The name Jeshurun means righteousness. How did their righteousness grow fat? What does Moses mean when he writes about strange gods and new gods who have come lately? Can we see any of these strange, new gods in our society today? If so how do we confront them?

Picturing the Passage

Draw a picture of yourself as God's warrior!

Activity for Lesson Twelve

In this lesson we were talking about the power of faith. Our faith has the ability to tear down the strongholds of sin in our lives. For this activity, we will be playing the game "Walls of Jericho Bowling."

Materials:

- Ball used for bowling ball
- Boxes or any other object that can be stacked.
- These boxes/objects will be nocked down. Make sure there is nothing that can be broken.
- Paper
- Pen, pencils
- Tape
- Prizes

Procedure:

- Write name of each person who will be participating a paper.
- This paper will serve as a score sheet
- Assemble the pile of boxes/objects
- Stack them as high as you feel comfortable
- Mark a square using the tape on the floor.
- The square will indicate the area of scoring.
- Each person will take a turn trying to knock down the boxes which represent the walls of Jericho.
- Like bowling, each person gets two turns per frame.

- Score points for each box/object that is knocked outside of the taped off area.

- No points for any boxes/objects remaining inside the taped off square.

- This is why it is essential to mark off a square using tape.

- Play as many frames as time permits.

- Highest score wins.

Tribulation

Focus: **Read Isaiah 13:6-13** prior to beginning this study.

This day will come! The heavens and the earth will tremble as the Lord draws near to His day of vindication. For those who know Salvation, this is a day to rejoice! Our Savior, Jesus will set things in order, placing His throne within our midst and He will wipe away the tears of His children offering them eternal comfort (Rev. 21:3-5). What a blessed Hope we have in His appearing (Titus 2:13).

As this day draws near, He calls the church to prepare (Matthew 25:1-13). The children of God will be challenged to overcome increasing *pressure* to remain faithful to His Word. In the book of Matthew (24:9), Jesus uses the word *tribulation* to describe these coming trials. For this study, we will focus on the word *tribulation*. We will discover the definition of the word using Scripture. We will explore the purpose of *tribulation*. And finally, we will look to the hope resulting from the *tribulation*. This topic is difficult and at first mention probably brings a sense of foreboding to your ears. But take heart because we serve a Living God who offers us peace in His presence (John 16:33)! To God be the Glory, for great things He has done! Let us all rejoice!

The Inspiration for the Study found in Matthew 24:3-14

Read Mathew 24:3-14

1. What things will lead up to the *tribulation* that Jesus speaks of in verse 9? (Verses 4-8)

2. Where does this hatred of God's people come from? (verse 9)

In verse 9, Jesus says that there will be some who will be delivered up to *tribulation.* The hatred of the things of God from the secular culture will be the catalyst that brings *tribulation* to the church. As I stated earlier, this term is one of foreboding. It can fill us with the sense of impending doom as we read passages of Scripture that describe end-time events. The purpose of this study is not to strike fear, but to equip the church to trust in the Lord who fights for us (Exodus 14:14). To help us see what the Lord is truly saying in His use of the word *tribulation,* it is helpful to know the actual definition of the word.

The Greek word that is translated *tribulation* is: **θλῖψις** (G2347, thlipsis). The definition of the word in the Greek:
1. a pressing, pressing together, pressure
2. metaph. oppression, affliction, tribulation, distress, straits

We can see that the initial definition of the word is pressing or pressure. The secondary definition is where we find the words that cause us to experience apprehension at the things yet to come. But this word does not need to cause us to feel anxious. As we go through the study, I pray that you will be filled with the hope we can find in the Lord as we discover what *tribulation* is meant to be for those who believe.

Before we move on, I want to share a thought with you from one of my professors, Dr. Justin Elwell. In one of his messages, he was commenting about knowing the secret to the meaning of life. He quoted the book of **Job chapter 38 verses 39-41.** Read those verses now.

At first glance, it seems as if these verses have nothing to do with the meaning of life. What does the appetite of young lions or nourishing ravens have to do with our lives? In context, God is demonstrating that He is the One who ultimately has the self-sufficiency to take care of His creation. But what is the purpose of God's provision? What spiritual truth are we to draw from the young lions and the ravens? How does this provision point to the meaning of life for us as humans? Dr. Elwell suggests, using this illustration of the appetites of young lions and the nourishment of the ravens, that the meaning of life is to be filled. Like the bellies of the lions and ravens we are to be filled.

John 12:50 Life of fullness

3. What sort of life is Jesus offering?

The word in the Greek translated as life, in this verse is, **ζωή** (G2222, Zoe). The definition of this word is:

"Of absolute fulness of life, both essential and ethical, which belongs to God, and through Him both to the hypostatic "logos" and to Christ in whom the "logos" put on human nature."

Let me explain further. Dr. Elwell connected the verses in Job with the account of Jacob and Esau. Turn to **Genesis 25:27-34.** Read the verses.

4. In verse 32, what does Esau claim will happen to him because of his hunger?

In this context, Esau equated hunger to death. Because his belly was empty, Esau could think of nothing but to be filled, to get food at any cost. An empty stomach results in death. A full stomach equals life. This is a very concrete, yet profound view of the meaning of life. Think for a moment about both the physical and spiritual connotation.

The physical picture of having a full belly is to be full of life. To have an empty belly is to be full of death or emptiness.

The spiritual understanding is to seek fullness in the spirit through the provision of God. When we are being filled by God spiritually, we are full of life. If we reject this infilling of God spiritually, we choose to embrace emptiness or death.

The meaning of life is to be full or filled by the mercy of God as He pours His Spirit out upon those who choose to accept His provision. Like the Israelites in the wilderness, God provided food and water but they still had to accept the gift of His mercy. Yet this provision was temporary. In faith, we can choose to be filled with nourishment that is eternal. Jesus is the Bread of Life and Living Water that will never perish (John 6:35).

The **warning** we are to draw from the analogy of Esau selling his birthright is essential to understand for out spiritual health and the health of the church. This relates to a danger associated with *tribulation*.

5. What was Esau willing to do because of hunger?

6. What did Esau give up as the first-born son of Isaac?

7. What is the danger for the people of God if we are not being filled? Or in other words, what could happen if we allow ourselves to go hungry, spiritually?

8. What is the consequence if we sell our birthright?

9. What then do we need to continually strive to do as believers?

10. What is church leadership responsible to do?

We can see that it is imperative that we seek to be filled through the study of the Word so that we do not act impulsively. You can draw your own conclusions as to what it means to sell your birthright as a Christian. At the very least, if we are not seeking daily to press into God, we run the risk of not carrying out His will in our lives. We will be rejecting our responsibility to be witnesses to the mercy of God to the next generation. This brings us back to the concept of tribulation.

Matthew 24:9-13: Tribulation, social pressure seeking to change the people of God.

11. Where is the *tribulation/pressure* coming from in verse 9?

12. What is this *pressure* attempting to do to the people of God? (verse 10).

13. As social pressures increase against the church, what will grow cold? (verse 12).

14. What do we have to do in order to not allow our love to grow cold? (verse 13).

15. How do we endure? (hint, we have to avoid the same fate ae Esau).

It is vital that we seek to remain filled through the Word of God in these times if trial. I am surprised at how quickly things have changed due to our current situation. If we are not actively seeking the Lord in our quarantined, daily lives, we run the risk of falling victim to spiritual hunger. The question we have to ask ourselves is, '**How will the church continue to be filled in times like**

this?' This is not a question that is easy to answer. I think it is therefore imperative that we begin having conversations now so that we are prepared for next time. Think about how we can, as the church, continue to fill our brothers and sisters in times of famine and share these ideas with others.

Matthew 13:1-9 Parable of the soils

16. In order for the seed to take root, what needed to be prepared? (verse 8)

17. In our spiritual lives, in order for the seed of the Gospel to take root, what needs to be prepared?

18. Who should we be preparing to be 'good soil?'

Matthew 13:18-23 explanation of the parable

19. In verse 21, why was the seed not able to have a firm root?

20. What caused the root to be taken away?

The word *affliction* in verse 21 is the Greek word *thlipsis* which is sometimes translated as *tribulation*.

21. Why does *affliction/tribulation* come against the seed planted in rocky places?

22. What are we to learn because of the *tribulation* that will come because of the Word?

We must be diligent to prepare our own soil and the soils of others so that we do not sell our birthright or fall away because of the affliction striking at us.

Matthew 7:24-27 Parable of the Two Builders

23. On whose house does the rain fall?

24. What prevented the wise man's house from being washed away?

25. What caused the wise man to find protection in times of *tribulation?* (verse 24).

26. Why did the foolish man's house fall?

Sand is like the words of men; it is unstable and everchanging. If we build our faith upon the words of men, we build on shaky ground. We build upon ever-changing cultural norms. We must take the warnings of God seriously and build upon His Word. His word is unchanging, and eternal. We must act in response to His Word, preparing ourselves to be ready for *tribulation*.

The purpose of Pressure or Tribulation

Hosea 5:9-15 The Rebuke of Apostacy

Ephraim refers to the Northern Kingdom in Israel. The name means "doubly fruitful." They were not living up to their name. Judah refers to the Southern Kingdom. This name means "praised." Unfortunately, Judah was not praising they were seeking praise.

27. What was Judah accused of? (verse 10).

28. What did Ephraim follow? (verse 11).

29. What is the purpose of the affliction? (verse 15).

Tribulation/Affliction in this context was poured against Ephraim and Judah in an effort to draw them back to the knowledge of God. *Affliction* was meant to cause the people to seek God. This is not meant to be punishment, but in essence a form of grace leading the people back to Him. When God convicts our hearts, it is not meant to be a burden but an outpouring of His Grace.

30. What do we need to turn away from? Is the Lord pouring out *affliction* to cause us to seek Him?

Zechariah 13 Purification by the Lord

In this chapter, God is instructing His people to rid themselves of all that attempts to draw them away from the purity of the Holy Word. God will do some of the purification on His own, but He will also require **us** to cut off things that draw us away from truth. We have partial responsibility to seek God in purity of heart. This does not earn us merit or solidify our salvation. It is simply a response to God in love and a way to preserve the witness of God for generations to come.

31. What is the purpose of tribulation in verse 9?

32. When we call upon God, what is His response?

James 1:1-4 The Profit of Trial

33. What is a bond-servant?

34. What do trials produce? (verse 3)

35. Why do we need endurance? (Ephesians 6:11)

36. What is the perfect result of endurance? (verse 4)

37. What is God's standard of perfection? **(Genesis 17:1-2)**.

1 Peter 1:3-19 Our Inheritance through Tribulation

38. What inheritance are we given in faith and how is it described? (verses 3-5).

39. Why is our inheritance imperishable?

40. Where is it reserved?

41. What are we protected by? (verse 5).

42. Now is the time of distress, as Peter writes in verse 6. What should our response be?

43. What are the trials in verse 6 supposed to produce? (verse 7).

44. When our faith is *proved*, what is it more precious than? Why?

45. Who is given praise and glory when our faith is tested? (verse 7).

46. What is the outcome of our faith? (verse 9)

47. What do the angels contemplate in verse 12?

48. What are we to be doing in verse 13?

49. Does this sound like we are to be waiting around to see what happens and then react to things as they fall upon us?

50. What does God expect of us in verse 15?

51. What is holiness? Can we achieve it?

Holiness is the presence of God within us. It is not a standard that we are to try and achieve. It is not a destination but an expression of Hope and Grace and Mercy of the Living God dwelling within the Tabernacle of flesh. Holiness is our willingness to allow God to work through us and in us.

52. Why are we to conduct ourselves in fear? (verse 17).

53. How are we redeemed? (verse 18, 19).

Romans 5: 1-5 Exaltation in *Tribulation*

54. What are the two instances that Paul tells us to be exulted or joyful? (verses 2 and 3)

55. What is the purpose of *tribulation?*

56. Summarize the purpose of those times we experience *tribulation/pressure.*

The hope of *pressure/tribulation* resulting in His appearing

John 16:16-22 What is the thing He tells us

57. In verse 20, why does Jesus say the disciples will weep but the world will rejoice?

In verse 21, the word *anguish* resulting from the labor of a mother is the Greek word *thlipsis.* Jesus used the *tribulation/anguish* experienced during the birth of a baby to describe the result of the trial. Through *tribulation/anguish* we can find joy, like the birth of a newborn. What more joy could there be knowing that present *tribulation* will result in an imperishable life. The hope of Salvation is born through *tribulation.*

58. Why can our heart rejoice? (verse 22).

59. Who can take away this joy? (verse 22)

John 16:32-33 The Overcomer of the World

60. Why did Jesus tell the disciples that they would be scattered?

61. Where does the *tribulation* that causes people to scatter come from?

62. Does Jesus tell us that we will escape *tribulation?*

63. Why should we remain hopeful in times of *affliction?* (verse 33)

Acts 14:19-22 Entering the Kingdom

64. Did Paul face *tribulation?*

65. Did the difficulties that Paul faced cause him to give up his faith or reject his calling?

66. How did Paul respond to *tribulation?*

67. What is the result of *tribulation?* (verse 22)

68. How are we to respond to *tribulation?*

69. What is the result of our endurance? (verse 22)

Romans 8: 33-39 Who can separate us from the love of Jesus

70. Who intercedes on our behalf? (verse 34)

71. Who is able to condemn us? (verse 33)

72. Does *tribulation* or distress or anything else have the power to separate us from our Savior? (verse 35)

73. How do we overwhelmingly conquer? (verse 37)

74. Name the things that **do not have the power** to cause us to be separated from the love of Jesus. (verse 38-39)

75. Can we have confidence in His salvation?

2 Corinthians 4: 15-18 Momentary Light *Affliction*

76. Why does Paul tell us that this light *affliction* is momentary?

I want to take a moment to point out the word that is translated *affliction*. In the Greek, the word that Paul uses is *thlipsis*. Paul is encouraging that the *tribulation* that we face in this present world is temporary. Though, many of us face extremely difficult things in our lives, we are to take heart in the knowledge that these *afflictions* are temporary. We are looking forward to an eternal hope in the restoration that lies ahead. I know things can get overwhelming, but know that we are the children of a God who loves us and He watches over us.

77. What is the result of *affliction?*

The word Paul uses for weight in his statement 'weight of glory' is the Greek word, **βάρος** (G922, Baros). Surprisingly the word can be translated as *burden*.

78. What do you think Paul is trying to tell us when he says that '*affliction* produces and eternal weight or *burden* of glory? Is God's glory a *burden*?

Remember *tribulation* means *pressure*. We have already discovered the result of *pressure* from both the secular world as well as the *pressure* applied by God. The intend result of *tribulation* is to refine and press us to prepare.

Paul is telling us in verse 17 of 2 Corinthians 4 that temporary *affliction* results in the weight of Gods glory to bear down upon us. We are being prepared to experience a reality in the Kingdom of God that is beyond our comprehension.

One other thought, Paul says we will experience the weight of God's glory. He uses a word in Greek that can be translated as burden.

79. What would the burden of God's glory pressure us to do as we live out this life?

80. How can we overcome the battle in our minds when we are experiencing *affliction?* (verse 18)

C.S. Lewis writes of the burden of expressing God's glory to the lost in his book entitled: "The Weight of Glory." I will briefly quote an expert from this book to direct our thoughts to what is the burden of glory we are discussing.

"It is a serious thing to live in a society of possible gods and goddesses, to remember that the dullest and most uninteresting person you can talk to may one day be a creature which, if you say it now, you would be strongly tempted to worship, or else a horror and a corruption such as you now meet, if at all in a nightmare. All day long we are, in some degree, helping each other to one or the other of these destinations. It is in the light of these overwhelming possibilities, it is with the awe and the circumspection proper to them, that we should conduct all our dealings with one another, all friendships, all loves, all play, all politics. There are no ordinary people. You have never talked to a mere mortal. Nations, cultures, arts, civilizations- these are mortal, and their life is to ours as the life of a gnat. But it is immortals whom we joke with, work with, marry, snub, and exploit- immortal horrors or everlasting splendours."[3]

The *burden* of glory is found in our witness to His Glory. Paul writes of the drive born of knowing God. This knowledge should cause us to live for Him as His earthly witness resulting in seeking His holiness. Not for our glory, but for the salvation of the lost and His Glory. As we draw closer to God, this world becomes a fragment of time in the vastness of that which is God. It is therefore imperative that we use this time for His glory. This is the *burden of glory.* This is the weight that bears upon us as we live out our lives. We must *speak **life*** into those with whom we come into contact, the immortals, as C.S. Lewis puts it. Our witness as the children of God is to carry His Light to the lost. We should

---

[3] Lewis, C.S. *The Weight of Glory and Other Addresses* (Harper One, New York, NY): 45

be *burdened by His Glory* to do so. We should be just as *burdened* to pass on the knowledge of God to our children. This is the responsibility of every parent. We must be the example of walking out our faith to our children. It is not just the Pastor or Sunday School teacher's responsibility. It is our responsibility. Additionally, we cannot just give our children over to the culture. As we have learned, the drive of the secular culture if to afflict the church with *tribulation* in an attempt to cause some to fall away. We must make our faith real and central in our homes so that our children will be equipped to withstand the trials that lie ahead.

Tribulation and the result of undergoing hardships should cause us to press into God. *Tribulation* should solidify our desire to carry out the call of our faith. Without this pressure, we become lazy. It is not very hard to name things that we are lazy about accomplishing in our lives. When the pressure to get something done is not felt, we often procrastinate. A result of *tribulation* is to help us all stay sharp in our faith and to prepare us for the next time *tribulation* comes.

Hebrews 12:1-10 Enduring Discipline

81. Who should we fix our eyes upon as we run with endurance? (verse 2)

82. Why should we fix our eyes on Jesus?

83. Who does God discipline?

84. If you feel convicted in your heart, where is it coming from?

85. In what should this conviction give us confidence?

Hebrews 12:18-29 The Holy Mountain

86. Where has our faith taken us? (verse 22)

87. Why does the blood of Jesus speak better than the blood of Abel? (verse24)

Abel's blood cries from the ground (Genesis 4:10). Abel was not resurrected. Abel was condemned to suffer death as a result of sin. Jesus rose from the dead. His blood is not bound to the earth. The blood of Jesus speaks from heaven. This is why the blood of Christ speaks better. It is because under the covering of His blood we can be resurrected unto newness of life.

88. What does the voice of Jesus calling forth from the heavens do? (verse 26)

89. What will be removed by this shaking?

90. Where will it be removed from?

91. What will remain? (verse 27 and 28)

92. What cannot be shaken?

93. In the knowledge of His unshakable Kingdom, what is our response? (verse 28)

94. How can we show gratitude to the Lord?

Colossians 3:15-17 Showing Gratitude to God

"Let the peace of Christ rule in your hearts, since as members of one body you were called to peace. And be thankful. Let the message of Christ dwell among you richly as you teach and admonish one another with all wisdom through psalms, hymns, and songs from the Spirit, singing to God with gratitude in your hearts. And whatever you do, whether in word or deed, do it all in the name of the Lord Jesus, giving thanks to God the Father through him."

The effect of *Tribulation/Pressure* results in a wonder that is more precious that gold and sweeter than honey. This is the Lord's will for tribulation that falls upon the saints. Take heart because He seeks to perfect you in your faith to rest in the peace of our Savior. Under the covering of His blood, we are given the promise of eternal life in His Kingdom. The Lord uses *tribulation* to refine us. Though it is difficult at times, all things work to the Glory of God (Romans 11:36).

One last word of encouragement. I often think of *tribulation* in terms of a basketball. Imagine a basketball. All around the outside of the ball, air is pressing down. The ball is surrounded by external *pressure* or *tribulation,* if you will. The external pressure will cause the ball to go flat if not for what? Internal pressure. The ball is also filled with internal pressure that is greater than the external pressure trying to cause it to go flat. Not only that, the internal pressure is the reason that the ball is able to bounce. The greater the internal pressure, the higher the ball will bounce.

Brothers and Sisters, we will face *tribulation.* We will face *pressure.* The *pressure/tribulation* is external. We are pressed upon by many things and these things will attempt to flatten us. But our hope is found in the One who resides within us. Beloved, we have a far greater presence dwelling within us who pushes back with insurmountable *pressure.* Our Savior will not be overcome and the *pressure* that He exerts on our behalf will never cease nor diminish. There is no *tribulation* that we will ever face that will catch Jesus off guard or cause Him to stumble. The greater the world pushes against His children, the more intensely He will push back.

Have faith, hope in the One who Saves and Maranatha, (Jesus has come and Jesus is coming)!

Picturing the Passage

Draw a picture of that illustrates the result of tribulation.

Activity for Lesson Thirteen

In this lesson we participated in a word study centered around the term *tribulation*. We learned the Biblical definition of tribulation. We also learned that there are times when we will go through periods of tribulation in our lives. It is often the case in these times that the Lord is trying to encourage us to grow in faith. The activity for this lesson will require homework. Additionally, I pray that this activity serves to offer you hope and possible develop within you the practice of journaling. When we take the time to journal and reflect on the things that the Lord is doing in our lives, in most cases we are able to see Him working.

Materials:

- Journal (for each participant in the study). Whatever type of notebook, journal, tablet that you find will be sufficient.
- Markers; pencils; pens; scissors; Glue
- Various scrapbooking papers
- Any other material that is available to help decorate the cover of the journal.

Procedure:

- Begin by taking a moment to discuss the value in journaling.
- Maybe provide a few examples of journaling.
- Suggest that part of the journaling experience can involve copying Bible verses.
- Allow time for the group to develop an idea for the cover.
- Allow time to begin constructing the cover.
- For the first journal entry: think about a time of tribulation in your life.
- Write on how you can now see that God was working in that time of trial.

The Great Commission

16 But the eleven disciples proceeded to Galilee, to the mountain which Jesus had designated. 17 When they saw Him, they worshiped Him; but some were doubtful. 18 And Jesus came up and spoke to them, saying, "All authority has been given to Me in heaven and on earth. 19 Go therefore and make disciples of all the nations, baptizing them in the name of the Father and the Son and the Holy Spirit, 20 teaching them to observe all that I commanded you; and lo, I am with you always, even to the end of the age.

Matthew 28:16-20 NASB95

About the Author

Corby Shuey is married to his lovely wife Kelly. They have two daughters and they live in Lebanon, PA. They enjoy spending time together, walking in God's creation and playing board games. Corby serves as the Senior Pastor of a church located in Lebanon County, Pennsylvania. An archive of messages can be found on the church website. He is a graduate of Biblical Life College and Seminary. He holds a Master of Divinity degree. Corby is an author. He publishes blogs on his website, corbyshuey.com. He has also written a number of books and Bible studies. The books can be found on his website or on Amazon.com by searching his name.